W9-DDN-975

Praise for the first edition of *A Mind of Its Own*

'We are all vain bigots, thanks to the foibles of the human brain, so argues Fine in her witty survey of psychology experiments ... An ideal gift for anyone interested in psychology' *Focus*

'Filled with quotable stories and interactive ways of how our brain has a buoyant ego of its own and is not the objective tool we might like to believe' *Bookseller*

'A light and amusing introduction to the brain and how it works on our perceptions and actions' *Publishing News*

'Consistently well-written and meticulously researched' Alain de Botton, *Sunday Times*

'In breezy demotic, Fine offers an entertaining tour of current thinking ... [she] is especially fascinating on the blurring of the line between pathological delusions and the normal deluded brain' *Telegraph*

'Fine with a sharp sense of humour and an intelligent sense of reality, slaps an Asbo on the hundred billion grey cells that – literally – have shifty, ruthless, self-serving minds of their own.' *The Times*

'Fine's style is chirpy ... [with] many affectionately amusing scenes' *Guardian*

'Fine sets out to demonstrate that the human brain is vainglorious and stubborn. She succeeds brilliantly.' *Mail on Sunday*

'Fine's flair for the humorous and anecdotal makes this a delightful read.' *Irish Times*

'Witty and informative' Philip Pullman

'Clear, accessible writing makes her a science writer to watch.' *Metro*

'Engaging, intelligent' *Scotland on Sunday*

'This is one of the most interesting and amusing accounts of how we think we think – I think.' Alexander McCall Smith

'A fascinating, funny, disconcerting and lucid book. By the end you'll realise that your brain can (and does) run rings around you.' Helen Dunmore

'A fun introduction to some of the factors that can distort our reasoning. I'd recommend it to anyone who is just getting interested in the topic, or as a gift for anyone you know who still thinks that their personal point of view is unprejudiced and reliable.' *Psychologist*

'Fine is that rare academic who's also an excellent writer. Highly recommended for all public and undergraduate libraries.' *Library Journal*

'Remarkably entertaining' *Los Angeles Times*

'Fine has got it just right. Although she is an academic, she writes like a human being ... All in all this short and enjoyable book is a must for anyone who wants to get a better understanding of what their brain gets up to when they aren't watching it. First class.' Brian Clegg, popularscience.co.uk

A MIND OF
ITS OWN

A MIND OF ITS OWN

CORDELIA FINE

HOW YOUR BRAIN DISTORTS AND DECEIVES

ICON

This edition published in the UK in 2007
by Icon Books Ltd, Omnibus Business Centre,
39–41 North Road, London N7 9DP
email: info@iconbooks.com
www.iconbooks.com

Previously published in 2005 by Icon Books Ltd

Sold in the UK, Europe and Asia
by Faber & Faber Ltd, Bloomsbury House,
74–77 Great Russell Street, London WC1B 3DA

Distributed in the UK, Europe and Asia
by Grantham Book Services,
Trent Road, Grantham NG31 7XQ

Distributed in South Africa
by Jonathan Ball, Office B4, The District,
41 Sir Lowry Road, Woodstock 7925

Distributed in Australia and New Zealand
by Allen & Unwin Pty Ltd,
PO Box 8500, 83 Alexander Street,
Crows Nest, NSW 2065

ISBN: 978-1840467-98-7

Typesetting by Wayzgoose

Printed and bound in the UK by
Clays Ltd, St Ives plc

Contents

Acknowledgements

My sincere thanks go to Simon Flynn and his colleagues at Icon Books for their assistance, in so many ways, with this book. Their contribution is greatly appreciated. I am also most grateful to my agent Barbara Lowenstein and her colleagues, for their advice and support on so many matters. Thanks, too, go to my editors at W.W. Norton for all they did for the US version of the book. For my mother, who always said just the right thing when I needed encouragement, I have the deepest gratitude. And finally, without my husband's very practical support, I would still be working on Chapter 1. Thank you.

Cordelia Fine is a Professor of the History and Philosophy of Science at the University of Melbourne. She is the author of the much-acclaimed *Delusions of Gender* (Icon, 2010), described as 'fun, droll yet deeply serious' by *New Scientist,* and of *Testosterone Rex: Unmaking the Myths of Our Gendered Minds* (Icon, 2017), winner of the 2017 Royal Society Insight Investment Science Book Prize, about which the judges said, 'Every man and woman should read this book ... an important, yet wickedly witty, book.'

Introduction

Do you feel that you can trust your own brain? So maybe it falters for a moment, faced with the thirteen times table. It may occasionally send you into a room in search of something, only to abandon you entirely. And, if yours is anything like mine, it may stubbornly refuse to master the parallel park. Yet these are petty and ungrateful gripes when we consider all that our brains actually do for us. Never before have we been made so aware of the extraordinary complexity and sophistication of those one hundred billion brain cells that make up the engine of the mind. And barely a day goes by when these gathered neurons aren't exalted in a newspaper article highlighting a newly discovered wonder of their teamwork.

From day to day, we take our brains somewhat for granted, but (particularly with this book in hand) it's likely that you're feeling a little quiet pride on behalf of your own. And, reading books on the subject of its own self aside, what else can't the thing do? After all, it tells you who you are, and what to think, and what's out there in the world around you. Its ruminations, sensations and conclusions are confided to you and you alone. For absolutely everything you know about anything, it is the part of yourself you have to thank. You might think that, if there's one thing in this world you can trust, it's your own brain. You are, after all, as intimate as it is possible to be.

But the truth of the matter – as revealed by the quite extra-ordinary and fascinating research described in this book – is that your unscrupulous brain is entirely undeserving of your confidence. It has some shifty habits that leave the truth distorted and disguised. Your brain is vainglorious. It's emotional and immoral. It deludes you. It is pigheaded, secretive and weak-willed. Oh, and it's also a bigot. This is more than a minor inconvenience. That fleshy walnut inside your skull is all you have in order to know yourself and to know the world. Yet, thanks to the masquerading of an untrustworthy brain with a mind of its own, much of what you think you know is not quite as it seems.

CHAPTER 1

The Vain Brain

For a softer, kinder reality

A week after Icon commissioned this book, I discovered that I was pregnant with my second child. The manuscript was due three days before the baby. My husband, a project manager both by temperament and employ, drew up a project plan for me. To my eye, it entirely failed to reflect the complexity, subtlety, and unpredictability of the process of writing a book. It was little more than a chart showing the number of words I had to write per week, and when I was going to write them. It also had me scheduled to work every weekend until the baby was born.

'This plan has me scheduled to work every weekend until the baby is born', I said.

'Plus all the annual leave from your job', my husband added.

I felt that he had missed the point. 'But when do I *rest*?'

'Rest?' My husband pretended to examine the plan. 'As I see it, you rest for two days after you finish the manuscript, shortly before going into labour, giving birth and having your life entirely taken over by the nutritional demands of a newborn.'

I had a brief image of myself in labour, telling the midwife between gasps of gas what a treat it was to have some time to myself.

'What if I can't do it?' I asked.

My husband gave me a 'this really isn't difficult' look. '*This* is how you do it', he said, stabbing the plan. 'You write this many words a week.'

He was right, I told myself. Of course I could do it. It was irrelevant that I was pregnant. After all, growing a baby is easy – no project plan required. My first trimester nausea and exhaustion would soon pass. The brains of other, weaker women might be taken hostage by pregnancy hormones, but not my brain. My bump would remain well enough contained to enable me to reach the computer keyboard. And absolutely, definitely, without a doubt, the baby would not come inconveniently early. Of course I could write the book.

I then did something very foolish. I began research on this chapter – the vain brain. The vain brain that embellishes, enhances and aggrandises you. The vain brain that excuses your faults and failures, or simply rewrites them out of history. The vain brain that sets you up on a pedestal above your peers. The vain brain that misguidedly thinks you invincible, invulnerable and omnipotent. The brain so *very* vain that it even considers the letters that appear in your name to be more attractive than those that don't.[1]

I didn't want to know any of this. But then it got worse. I went on to read just how essential these positive illusions are. They keep your head high and your heart out of your boots. They keep you from standing atop railway bridges gazing contemplatively at approaching trains. Without a little deluded optimism, your immune system begins to wonder whether it's worth the effort of keeping you alive. And, most extraordinary, it seems that sometimes your vain brain manages to transform its grandiose beliefs into reality. Buoyed by a brain that loves you like a mother, you struggle and persevere – happily blind to your own inadequacies, arrogantly dismissive of likely obstacles – and actually achieve your goals.

I needed my vain brain back. *Immediately.*

Luckily, I managed to regain my optimism, and the manuscript was delivered a few days before the baby. About three months later, however, my agent contacted me with the news that the US publisher W. W. Norton was interested in the book. In fact, they liked it so much that they wanted another hundred pages of it. (My husband didn't know which to open first – the champagne, or the spreadsheet.) This was a daunting prospect: just writing a shopping list can take all day when there is a small baby in the house. Thankfully, though, my positive illusions triumphed once again. Pushing aside all dispiriting thoughts of the difficulties ahead, I began to sharpen the pencils. And, as the existence of this new, longer version of the book proves, again, it worked for me. But now it's time for me to attempt to spoil your chances of happiness, health and success by disillusioning you.

While it troubles philosophers, for the rest of us it is vastly more comfortable that we can only know ourselves and the world through the distorting lens of our brains. Freud suggested that the ego 'rejects the unbearable idea', and since then experimental psychologists have been peeling back the protective layers encasing our self-esteem to reveal the multitude of strategies our brains use to keep our egos plump and self-satisfied. Let's start with some basic facts. When asked, people will modestly and reluctantly confess that they are, for example, more ethical, more nobly motivated employees, and better drivers than the average person.[2] In the latter case, this even includes people interviewed in hospital shortly after extraction from the mangled wrecks that were once their cars. No one considers themselves to fall in the bottom half of the heap, and statistically, that's not possible. But in a sample of vain brains, it's inevitable.

For one thing, if it's at all possible then your brain will interpret the question in the way that suits you best. If I were asked how my driving compares with others, I would rate myself better than average without hesitation. My driving record at speeds above one mile per hour is flawless. Yet below this speed my paintwork, and any stationary object I am attempting to park near, are in constant peril. These expensive unions between the stationary and the near-stationary are so frequent that at one point I actually considered enveloping the vulnerable portions of my car in bubble-wrap. My mother, in contrast, can reverse with exquisite precision into a parking spot at whiplash speeds. On the other hand, she regularly rams into the back of cars that 'should have gone' at roundabouts. She, too, considers her driving to be superb. You begin to see how everyone is able to stake their claim to be in the superior half of the driving population. If the trait or skill that you're being asked about is helpfully ambiguous, you interpret the question to suit your own idiosyncratic strengths.[3]

Even if you are unambiguously hopeless in an area of life, your brain gets round this by simply diminishing the importance of that skill. I, for example, cannot draw. I am the artistic equivalent of being tone deaf. However, this doesn't bother me in the slightest because to my brain, drawing is an unnecessary extra. I can see that it would be useful if one were an artist, but in the same way that it's useful for a contortionist to be able to wrap his legs behind his head. Essential for a small minority, but nothing more than a showy party trick for everyone else.[4] And in a final clever enhancement of this self-enhancement, people believe that their weaknesses are so common that they should hardly even be considered weaknesses, yet their strengths are rare and special.[5]

What these strategies reveal is that a bit of ambiguity can be taken a very long way by a vain brain. The next technique in your brain's arsenal of ego defence exploits ambiguity to the full. When we explain to ourselves and others why things have gone well or badly, we prefer explanations that cast us in the best possible light. Thus we are quick to assume that our successes are due to our own sterling qualities, while responsibility for failures can often be conveniently laid at the door of bad luck or damn fool others. This self-serving bias, as it is known, is all too easy to demonstrate in the psychology lab.[6] People arbitrarily told that they did well on a task (for example, puzzle solving) will take the credit for it, whereas people arbitrarily told that they did badly will assign responsibility elsewhere, such as with their partner on the task. The brain is especially self-advancing when poor performance could deliver a substantial bruise to your ego.[7] People told that puzzle solving is related to intelligence are much more likely to be self-serving than those told that puzzle solving is just something that people who don't like reading books do on trains. The bigger the potential threat, the more self-protective the vain brain becomes. In a final irony, people think that others are more susceptible to the self-serving bias than they are themselves.[8] (Allow yourself a moment to take that sentence fully on board, should you need to.)

Thus when life or psychology researchers are kind enough to leave the reasons for success or failure ambiguous, the self-serving bias is readily and easily engaged to protect and nurture the ego. However, our vain brains aren't completely impervious to reality. No matter how partial my explanation of why I added up the restaurant bill incorrectly, I have no intention of applying for any professorships in mathematics. In a way, this is definitely good. When we lose all sight of our ugly face in reality's mirror, this generally means that we have also lost grip on our sanity. But on the other hand, who wants to see the warts and all with pristine clarity? We've already seen how the vain brain casts our features at their most flattering angle. Now we'll rummage deeper into its bag of tricks. For by calling on powerful biases in memory and reasoning, the brain can selectively edit and censor the truth, both about ourselves and the world, making for a softer, kinder and altogether more palatable reality.

Failure is perhaps the greatest enemy of the ego, and that's why the vain brain does its best to barricade the door against this unwelcome guest. The self-serving bias we've already encountered provides a few extra services to this end. One approach is to tell yourself that, in retrospect, the odds were stacked against you and failure was all but inevitable. Researchers have found that optimists in particular use this strategy, which has been dubbed 'retroactive pessimism', and it makes failure easier to digest.[9]

'Self-handicappers', as they are called, exploit the self-serving bias in a different way. In self-handicapping, the brain makes sure that it has a non-threatening excuse for failure, should it occur. If you can blame your poor performance in an intelligence test on your lack of effort, for example, then your flattering self-image of your intelligence and competence can remain unchallenged. Self-handicapping also enhances the sweetness of success when it occurs, creating a win-win situation for your ego. Drug use, medical symptoms, anxiety … they can all be used to shield the ego from failure. Take, for example, a group of students who reported suffering severe anxiety during tests. According to a trio of refreshingly brusque researchers, the brains of these devious strategists exploit their test anxiety, whenever they can, to serve ignoble ends.[10] The researchers gave their test-anxious students a difficult two-part test, purportedly a measure of general intelligence. In the interval between the two parts of the test, the students were asked to say how anxious they were feeling about the test, and how much effort they were putting into it. However, right before this survey, *some* of the students had their potential handicap snatched away from them. They were told that a remarkable feature of the test they were taking was that their score was impervious to anxiety and – no matter how nervous they were – their score would be an accurate measure of their intellectual ability.

This was cunning as well as mean. If a test-anxious student merely reports accurately how anxious she is feeling, with no self-serving motivations, it should make no difference to her whether she thinks that anxiety might reduce her score on the test – she should declare the same level of anxiety regardless. However, if test anxiety is used to protect self-esteem, then it will be important whether she thinks that anxiety offers a plausible excuse for poor performance on the test. If she thinks that scores are adversely affected by nerves, she will be tempted to protect herself against possible failure by claiming greater susceptibility to the jitters. This is exactly what the researchers found. Only students who thought that their anxiety offered its usual non-threatening excuse for low marks hoicked up their self-reports of anxiety. The other students, who knew that they wouldn't be able to blame their nerves, didn't bother. They did something else instead. In place of their handicap of choice, these students instead claimed to have made less effort on the test. It takes more than a few psychologists to stymie the cunning of a determinedly vain brain.

Even when your brain does accept responsibility when things go wrong, research shows that just a few days later it may have conveniently cast off the more unflattering explanations for failure. In one experiment investigating this phenomenon, male university students were given a task that supposedly assessed their 'manual dexterity and cognitive perception coordination'.[11] ('I'm handy and I'm coordinated.') You can of course imagine a male ego immediately wanting a piece of that pie. The students were randomly told either that they were dexterous virtuosos of cognitive perception or that, frankly, the average china shop proprietor would more warmly welcome a bull into their shop. The men were then asked either immediately afterwards or a few days later to explain why they had done well or badly on the test. The students whose vain brains were given a few days to edit the memory of the experiment were much more self-enhancing in their explanations of why they had succeeded or failed, in comparison with the students who were asked for their explanations straight away.

Memory is one of your ego's greatest allies, of course. Good things about ourselves tend to secure a firm foothold in the brain cells, while bad stuff – oopsie – has a habit of losing grasp and slipping away. Imagine being given a personality test, and then a list of behaviours that – according to the test – you are likely to perform. Would you later remember more negative behaviours (such as 'You would make fun of others because of their looks' and 'You would often lie to your parents') or more positive behaviours (such as 'You would help a handicapped neighbour paint his house' or 'You would keep secrets if asked to')? Intuitively you might think that the rather surprising predictions that you are likely to be unkind and untrustworthy would so jar with your generally positive self-concept that they would be more memorable. However, when researchers gave people a bogus personality test of this sort, this is not what they found.[12] Instead, it was the predictions of caring and honourable behaviours that stuck in people's memories. The reason was that their brains simply refused to allocate as much processing time to nasty predictions as to the nice ones. It seems that it is easier for a camel to pass through the eye of a needle than for negative feedback to enter the kingdom of memory.

Not only does memory collude with the brain in the information that it lets in but, as you might begin to fear, it also controls the information it lets out. All brains contain an enormous database of personal memories that bear on that perennially fascinating question 'Who am I?', or the self-concept. But the self-concept, psychologists have discovered, is conveniently self-shifting.[13] If the self-concept you are wearing no longer suits your motives, the brain simply slips into something more comfortable. The willing assistant in this process is memory. It has the knack of pulling out personal memories that better fit the new circumstances. Two Princeton researchers observed this metamorphosis directly, by tempting the vain brains of their volunteers with an attractive change of self-concept.[14] They asked a group of students to read one of two (fabricated) scientific articles. The first article claimed that an extroverted personality helps people to achieve academic success. The second article, handed out to just as many students, claimed instead that introverts tend to be more academically successful. You can guess what's going to happen. Imagine it. You're a vain brain. You're a vain brain at *Princeton*, for goodness' sake. Someone's offering you a shimmering, glittering, dazzling self-concept that says, 'Hey, world. *I* am going to make it.' A personality trait you've been told offers the crystal stairway to triumph might not be quite your size, but if you can make it fit with a bit of tweaking, you will. Whichever personality trait the students thought was the key to success, they rated themselves more highly as possessing.

What happens is that the vain brain calls in memory to make sure that the most attractive self-concept fits. From the enormous wardrobe of rich and complicated autobiographical events from your life, your memory brings to the fore those memories that best match the self-concept you are trying to achieve. When people are told that extroverts, say, tend to be more successful than shy and retiring types, it is the memories that bear out their sociable and outgoing natures that rush quickly and easily to consciousness.[15] And as we've already seen, memory keeps the gate at the front door as well. Give someone who's been told that one type of personality leads to success a bit of personality feedback, and she will remember much more of the feedback that shows that she possesses the supposedly more favourable attribute.[16]

The vain brain's other powerful protectorate is reasoning. This might seem a little odd. Isn't reasoning supposed to be the compass that guides us towards the truth, not saves us from it? It seems not, particularly when our ego is under attack. In fact, the best we can say of our gift for thinking in these circumstances is that we do at least recognise that conclusions cannot be drawn out of thin air; we need a bit of evidence to support our case. The problem is that we behave like a smart lawyer searching for evidence to bolster his client's case, rather than a jury searching for the truth.[17] As we've seen, memory is often the over-zealous secretary who assists in this process by hiding or destroying files that harbour unwanted information. Only when enough of the objectionable stuff has been shredded dare we take a look. Evidence that supports your case is quickly accepted, and the legal assistants are sent out to find more of the same. However, evidence that threatens reason's most important client – you – is subjected to gruelling cross-examination. Accuracy, validity and plausibility all come under attack in the witness stand. The case is soon won. A victory for justice and truth, you think, conveniently ignoring the fact that yours was the only lawyer in the courtroom.

Time now to watch your hot-shot lawyer in action. Imagine

there's a rumour afoot that certain things about you augur badly for how well you will do in your chosen profession. Your reputation is at risk, and your lawyer is engaged to defend you from this potential slander. This was the situation created in a study demonstrating that the client is always right. University students were asked to take part in an experiment to do with the reasons for success in law, medicine and business.[18] They were given fictitious descriptions of people who supposedly did well or badly at professional school. The sorts of attributes they read about were things like being the youngest or oldest child, being Catholic or Protestant, and having had a mother employed outside the home or a stay-at-home mother.

Now, say one of the students is the youngest child of a Catholic family whose mother stayed at home rearing her and her ten older siblings, and she longs to be a doctor. Then she reads about a successful doctor who is Catholic, the oldest child, and whose mother went out to work. Wouldn't it be nice if she could convince herself that the things she has in common with the successful doctor are what make for success, but that the things they differ on aren't important? This is just what happens. The student decides that a Catholic upbringing brings success, but that the other two factors are relatively unimportant. However, if the student had been told that the same person was *un*successful, suddenly her Catholicism would seem far less relevant (what could religion possibly have to do with it?), but birth order and mother's employment – the factors she differs on – would suddenly become crucial. Your hard-working lawyer constructs the most flattering and self-serving case it can from the available data.

The next step is the evaluation of evidence. When that evidence poses a threat to your ego, a good lawyer can always find fault. In one such experiment, high-school students were given an intelligence test.[19] Some of them were told that they had done well, others that they had done badly. All of them were also given a few pages to read containing arguments from scientists both for and against the validity of intelligence tests. Even though everyone was given the same information, the poor guinea pigs whose egos had been threatened by negative feedback decided that intelligence tests were a much cruder tool for measuring intellectual depths than did students who were told that they'd done brilliantly. Was this because memory had hidden the pro-intelligence test files? Actually, no. In fact, the ego-threatened students remembered *more* of the pro-intelligence test arguments than did the others. This seems a little odd, until you consider all the effort the vain brain's lawyer must have put in to disparage those particular arguments. If you spend a great deal of effort cross-examining a witness you'll have a good memory for what they said, even if you don't believe a goddamn word of their lies.

On the whole, it seems we are content to employ the sloppiest of reasoning … until some threat to our motives appears, at which point we suddenly acquire the strictest possible methodological standards.[20] The smart lawyer inside us is also skilled at finding supporting witnesses to bolster our case. Remember the experiments in which people were told that being either outgoing or withdrawn by nature is more conducive to success? Well, your brain not only biases your memory to make you think that you've been blessed with the more favourable personality attribute. It also then encourages you to spend time in the company of people who think you're really like that.[21]

It's rather unsettling to know that your ego is so very well protected from reality. And it's not just your ego that's kept so safely removed from the truth. Perhaps understandably, given the slings and arrows of fortune we must dodge every day, your vain brain calls upon many of the same strategies to keep your perception of your future health, happiness and fortune pleasantly unrealistic.

Just as we all believe ourselves to be better people than average, so too we think ourselves relatively invulnerable to life's trials. As with anything that threatens our egos, we push absurdly high our standards for evidence that might challenge our rosy beliefs. For example, brains prefer not to have to take too seriously any medical information that challenges our sense of physical invincibility. My father-in-law enjoys a lifestyle that, to put it bluntly, would leave the hardiest of cardiologists weeping into their public health information pamphlets. Statistically, he should probably have died shortly before he was born. Concerning all those pesky 'smoking – disease – death connection' studies, he is breathtakingly (excuse the pun) dismissive. Yet he is not immune to the charms of scientific discovery when it suits. For example, he never fails to encourage me to push aside my tumbler of water in favour of a nice healthy glass of red wine. In an experimental study of this 'motivated scepticism' phenomenon, people were given an article to read that set out the medical dangers for women (but not men) of drinking too much coffee.[22] Men and women who drank little or no coffee found it convincing. Men who drank a lot of coffee found it convincing. There are no prizes for guessing which group thought the link between caffeine and disease unpersuasive.

Vain brains are reluctant to accept hints of physical vulnerability even when it's staring them in the face. In another demonstration of self-protective incredulity, some volunteers were told about a fictitious medical condition called thioamine acetylase (TAA) deficiency. [23] TAA deficient individuals, they were reliably informed, were 'relatively susceptible to a variety of pancreatic disorders' later in life. Then one by one the volunteers were led into a private room (or was it?) to test themselves for the condition, by dipping a special piece of test paper (or *was* it?) into a sample of saliva. Some of the volunteers were told that if their TAA levels were normal, the strip would remain yellow. They were the lucky ones. The rest of the volunteers were told that if their TAA levels were normal the strip would turn dark green. They were the unlucky ones. The test strip, being made of ordinary yellow paper, wasn't going to change colour no matter how much spit it encountered.

These 'TAA deficiency' volunteers, the ones who 'failed' the saliva reaction test, were determinedly optimistic about the perils of TAA deficiency. They reckoned that both TAA deficiency and pancreatic disease were far less serious and far more common than did people who 'passed' the test. Those volunteers who failed also rated the saliva reaction test as less accurate. Even more defensive was their behaviour while they were taking the saliva test. The researchers were secretly spying on them, of course, while it took place. Everyone had been told that colour change in the test paper took from 10 to 60 seconds, but was generally complete within 20. Volunteers were asked to pop their strips into an envelope as soon as the test was done. The supposedly deficient volunteers were much slower to do this, giving their yellow paper a generous extra half a minute or so to change colour, compared with the 'no deficiency' volunteers. What's more, the majority of the volunteers who failed engaged in some kind of illicit retesting to help their recalcitrant strips along. Some people used a fresh saliva sample. Others retested using a new strip. Some placed the strip directly onto their tongue. The strips were shaken, blown, wiped and saturated with enormous volumes of saliva. These unlucky volunteers didn't like their diagnosis and they were seeking second, third and fourth opinions on the matter.

Vain brains can even trick us into unconsciously manipulating the outcome of a medical diagnosis to make it more acceptable. To show this, a group of experimentees were asked to immerse their forearm in a vat of icy cold water (yes, painful) and to keep it there for as long as they could bear.[24] They had to do this both before and after physical exercise. Some volunteers were told that if they could keep their arm in the ice-water for longer after exercise, that was a sign of long life expectancy. The other volunteers were told the reverse. Although they weren't aware that they were doing so, the volunteers changed their tolerance for the cold water after exercise in whichever direction they'd been told predicted a long and healthy life. Of course, manipulating their tolerance in this way couldn't possibly affect actual life expectancy, but that's not really what's important to a vain brain.

The rose-tinted spectacles through which we scrutinise information about our health can also push back our inevitable demise to a more distant horizon. Despite being confronted with a precisely calculated actuarial estimate of time of departure, we blithely estimate that we will live about ten years longer than we are allotted by mere statistics.[25] I recently came across a website that, on the basis of a few pertinent pieces of information, furnishes you with your likely date of death. (For those with a morbid interest, or the need to make very long-term plans, the website is www.deathclock.com.) From this helpful website I learnt that I would die on Sunday, 10 May 2054 at the age of 79. 'That seems very young', I thought, and instantly gave myself another – well – ten years, mostly on the grounds that I have long eschewed sausage meat, a product which must surely substantially impair longevity. Indeed, it seems that whenever we gaze into the future we take care only to peep through pink-hued lenses. Who, at the wedding altar is thinking, 'Fifty-fifty chance of this working – let's keep our fingers crossed'? Possibly most of the congregation, but probably not the bride or groom. Remember our Catholic student who made up theories to explain why she was likely to succeed at medical school? In the same study the researchers showed that people use the same sort of self-serving speculations to persuade themselves that *their* marriage will be happy.[26]

Nor does the self-deceit stop with our dismissal of the possibility that there may be trouble ahead. We also have an inflated sense of control over what is to come. Take, for example, a task in which volunteers are asked to try to get a light to come on by pressing a button.[27] Volunteers are told that the button might control the light; in fact, the light comes on and off randomly and its illumination is entirely unrelated to what the volunteer does with the button. Yet although the volunteers have absolutely no control over the light, their perception is very different. They experience an illusion of control, as it is known, and claim to have an influence over the light. As subjects of future vanity, people rate their personal control more highly if the light happens to come on more often. In other words, we are even more susceptible to the self-flattering impression that we are responsible for how things have turned out, when they turn out well.

We also succumb more readily to a false sense of influence on occasions when a little omnipotence would be particularly helpful. Offer a hamburger as a prize in a random draw from a deck of cards, and hungry volunteers will optimistically persuade themselves of greater clout on the task than will volunteers who have already eaten.[28] And desperate times call for desperate delusions. In the painfully sleep-deprived months just after the birth of our second child I was convinced that I, and I alone, knew the best and quickest way to get the baby back to sleep. 'No, *no*!' I reprimanded my husband one afternoon, walking in on his attempt to settle the baby for a nap. 'You have to sit him on your lap with his back curved to the left and hum "Humpty Dumpty" while you stroke his forehead with your thumb. Really, it's the only thing that works.'

'Well, no wonder it takes you so long to get him to sleep', my husband replied with pitying scorn, 'because what he actually finds most soothing is to be walked up and down between the crib and the window with a gentle vertical rocking motion. Would you mind adjusting the blind on your way out? It needs to be raised to exactly two-and-a-half inches above the sill.'

When it comes to babies, an illusion of control is probably the best one can hope for.

The conceit that we show in our thinking about the future goes further still than self-aggrandising calculations about our own power and prospects. We are overly confident, too, that our favoured political parties or sports teams will be victorious. Ask a group of people who they *think* will win a forthcoming election, and then divide them up according to who they *hope* will win (the Conservative and Labour parties, say) and you see something rather curious. Labour supporters will be significantly more hopeful about the chances of the Labour party than Conservatives, and vice versa. And the more fervently you want your party to win, the higher you rate their chance of success.[29]

From where does this eternal hope spring? The sleazy lawyer may play a part, hiding or distorting unwelcome information. Yet even promises of cash prizes for accurate predictions – which should surely serve to counteract our predisposition to be unrealistic – can't rid us of our sanguine expectations. It is the same, too, in the sporting stadium. Even in the betting booth, where people put their hard-earned money where their mouth is, judgment is swayed by desire.[30] Another possible explanation for our undue positivism is that we are tempted into complacency by the company we keep; if everyone you know is a Democrat, their chances may begin to seem more hopeful than they really are.[31] Yet this cannot be the whole story. Even people with the most up-to-date polling information at their fingertips are susceptible to the 'wishful thinking' effect.[32]

We think it will be so, simply because we would prefer it to be so, the research suggests. This was made starkly clear in a laboratory study of wishful thinking in which the researcher randomly assigned college students to two teams, and then pitted the teams against one another in a dart-throwing competition.[33] As one person from each team stood ready, dart in hand, everyone else scribbled down a guess as to which of the two would throw closer to the bull's eye – the teammate or the opponent. Then the next two competitors stepped up for a throw-off. Their chances were rated by everyone else, and so on, until everyone had thrown a dart.

Although the teams were put together in an entirely haphazard fashion, the flame of fellow feeling was nonetheless sparked. When asked, the students confessed to a desire that their own team would triumph. And, in line with their desires, each team thought it more likely that their own team would prevail against the opposition. Not only that, but all but a few of the students were confident that their predictions about which team would win were unaffected by their hankering for their own team's victory. Yet what else could have been biasing their judgments, other than the hope that they would be on the winning side? Indeed, when the researcher took a closer look at the data, he found that the stronger the yearning, the greater the confidence. Hope springs eternally from hope, it seems.

As we draw towards the end of this chapter, there are two morals to be drawn. One, never trust a social psychologist. Two, never trust your brain. They both manipulate your perception of reality, thus tricking you into embarrassing vanities. (Of course, in the case of the social psychologist those vanities are then permanently recorded in order that other professionals may be entertained by them. So perhaps you should trust social psychologists even less than you do your brain.) But don't feel angry with your vain brain for shielding you from the truth. There is in fact a category of people who get unusually close to the truth about themselves and the world. Their self-perceptions are more balanced, they assign responsibility for success and failure more evenhandedly, and their predictions for the future are more realistic. These people are living testimony to the dangers of self-knowledge. They are the clinically depressed.[34]

Psychologist Martin Seligman and colleagues have identified a pessimistic 'explanatory style' that is common in depressed people.[35] When pessimists fail they blame themselves, and think that the fault is in themselves ('I'm stupid', 'I'm useless'), will last forever and will affect everything they do. This is a far cry from the sorts of explanations that happy, self-serving people give for failure.

What is more, it is becoming clear that pessimism can seriously endanger your physical, as well as your mental, health. The deathclock asks only four questions in order to calculate how many years to shear off your expected time of death. Are you male? Do you smoke? Are you overweight? And are you a pessimist? You may be surprised to see your personal disposition up there as a risk factor along with gender, smoking and obesity, but the research does seem to bear out its right to be in the Big Four.

In one remarkable study of the effect of mental outlook on longevity, researchers analysed brief autobiographies written more than seventy years ago by North American nuns about to take their final vows.[36] The researchers scrutinised the passages, counting how often the nun expressed a positive emotion. This yielded, for each nun, what one might (bearing the joyful heroine of *The Sound of Music* somewhat wryly in mind) refer to as a 'Maria measure'. The researchers then looked to see whether their emotional outlook was related to their lifespan. The statistics showed that the more cheerful a nun's autobiographical account, the longer the nun had on this earthly plain before being gathered up to the celestial empire. In fact, on average the jovial nuns lived almost a decade longer than their more sombre sisters.[37]

Indeed, a Maria-style outlook could be just the ticket when the dog bites or the bee stings. Thinking about raindrops on roses and whiskers on kittens in the face of adversity may help to subdue the damaging cardiovascular effects of sadness.[38] And the cheery Pollyannaism of optimists is matched by a similar can-do attitude in their immune systems.[39] Optimists make fewer doctor visits, are more likely to survive cancer, are less likely to suffer recurrent heart disease, and are less likely to meet with an untimely death.[40] Gloom merchants may find it hard to cultivate a more cheerful perspective in the face of such data, but it's certainly worth trying.

But while both our emotional and physical well-being seem to benefit from a careful filtering of the harsh light of reality, is there not a price to pay for being blinkered in this way? (Aside, that is, from the small matter of our self-knowledge turning out to be little more than an agreeable fiction.) Certainly, blind optimism can sometimes lead us astray. Our self-serving tendency to blame anything and anyone but ourselves for mistakes in our past can doom us to repeat them. This was the dismal conclusion of a study that asked college students to predict when they would finish an assignment they had just been set.[41] As we have all done ourselves on many occasions, the students seriously under-estimated how long it would take. Even asking the students to reflect on their failures to finish similar assignments in the time they had allotted themselves on previous occasions had no effect in challenging this immoderate confidence. The students simply dismissed those botch-ups as irrelevant; past assignments were late due to freakish obstacles that would surely never arise again.

This touching faith that we hold it in our gift to deliver on time, despite all evidence to the contrary, can leave nothing but chaos in its wake. The planning fallacy, as it is known, is familiar to us all: from the take-home work that lies untouched in our briefcase all weekend, to the years-long delays in completing local construction projects that have project managers reaching for their blood pressure pills.

Not only is time money, but we may also be forking out directly for the vain brain's sleight of hand. As they rake in their profits, bookkeepers and casinos should offer up fulsome thanks to the wishful thinking phenomenon. And if your salary happens to depend on your ability to predict the future, an illusion of con-trol can become an extremely expensive psychological luxury. Researchers asked a hundred traders from investment banks to play a computerised 'financial market' version of the 'press button/hope for light to come on' task.[42] (Instead of trying to get a light to come on, the traders had to try to increase an index value.) Afterwards, the traders filled in questionnaires about the game that revealed how readily they were seduced into the erroneous belief that they could control changes in the value of the index. Interestingly, the statistics showed that the more arrogant the trader about his influence on the computer task, the less he earned on the trading floor. According to the researchers' analyses, traders with a high score on the 'illusion of control' scale earned about £60,000 per annum less than traders with only average scores.[43]

Inevitably, our unrealistic expectations, and our reluctance to admit to our weaknesses and limits, will sometimes trip us up. However, the brain does have a helpful strategy in place to minimise such mishaps. So long as our minds are yet to be made up, we actually view ourselves and life unusually realistically as we quietly contemplate our future. Volunteers asked to deliberate a decision they had yet to make (to go on holiday, for example, or end a relationship) were less grandiose about themselves, more pensive, more attuned to the risks of life, and less susceptible to the illusion of omnipotence than were other volunteers not induced to be in such a contemplative frame of mind.[44] This 'window of realism' is presumably what keeps our aspirations from becoming too fanciful, our strivings too absurd.

Once our decision is made, however, the window of realism is snapped shut more tightly than ever before. Volunteers told to reflect on a decision that they had already made were even more exaggeratedly buoyant about themselves and their prospects than normal. And there is good reason for the vain brain to slip up into top gear just as soon as we are ready to put our plans into action.[45] The shamelessly immodest cry of the conceited brain – 'Sure! I can do that! (And if I can't it's someone else's fault …)' – is like a psychic trampoline. It propels you upwards, but provides a soft landing should you rapidly descend. The tricks of the vain brain enable you to pursue your ambitions while keeping your ego safe from harm. Self-handicappers, who protect their self-esteem by providing themselves in advance with a non-threatening reason for poor performance ('I didn't try', or 'I didn't study'), gain another benefit from this strategy. By buffering their delicate egos from potential failure in this way, self-handicappers can have a go at things, safe in the knowledge that they have an excuse on hand should things go badly. People who habitually protect their pride in this way were given the opportunity to self-handicap before playing a pinball machine.[46] By allowing the volunteers to choose how long to practise beforehand, the researchers were able to see how self-handicapping (by practising less) gave the volunteers the psychological leeway they needed to enjoy and persist at playing pinball, even when they were told that they weren't terribly good at it.

Ego-friendly excuses for unrealised aspirations are also invaluable in the classroom. Schoolchildren doing badly in reading or maths, when encouraged to blame their difficulties on lack of effort rather than lack of ability, show remarkable gains in both persistence and accomplishment.[47] And persuading yourself that the sun *will* come out tomorrow – that the setbacks you are experiencing are only temporary and nothing to do with any personal deficiencies – lends strength to persevere with your goals. First-year undergraduates worried about their poor grades were enticed by researchers into thinking that grades naturally improve after the first semester.[48] In a spectacular demonstration of the self-fulfilling prophecy, these students went on to get better grades (both a week and a year later), and were less likely to drop out, compared with similarly concerned students who were not persuaded to be optimistic about the future in this way.

We have many reasons, then, to be grateful to the brain for its careful stretching of the truth. Indeed, without our vain brains, would we even bother to get up in the morning? One final, glorious reason to thank your brain for its little white lies is that they make life itself endurable. According to the sensationally named Terror Management Theory, developed by a psychologist rejoicing in the surname Pyszczynski,[49] a healthily vain brain is 'a protective shield designed to control the potential for terror that results from awareness of the horrifying possibility that we humans are merely transient animals groping to survive in a meaningless universe, destined only to die and decay'. I'm sure you will agree that if a few positive illusions can keep at bay the disturbing thought that in truth you are of no more significance in the universe than, as Pyszczynski cruelly puts it, 'any individual potato, pineapple, or porcupine', then we all owe a large debt of gratitude to our vain brains.

But let's end on a more comforting note. Although in the grand scheme of things you may not be of more significance than a porcupine, you are almost certainly a better driver.

CHAPTER 2

The Emotional Brain

Sweaty fingers in all the pies

My son, thirteen months old, is crying as if his heart will break. He sobs with his entire body, and I know that in a few seconds he will assume what my husband and I call 'The Tragedy Pose'. Sure enough, soon he collapses onto the floor and flops forward so that his forehead hits the carpet. I am holding in my hand the accomplice to the act that has obliterated all joy from my son's existence. This object and I, between us, have left no other course available to my young child but to give himself over completely to unmitigated, carpet-drenching grief. I struggle painfully but successfully with the urge to ruin his character forever by returning to him this item upon which, clearly, his entire happiness depends. It is a ballpoint pen.

As it happens, I know just how it feels to have ballpoint pens taken away. My husband, as part of his Stationery Stationing System, has strategically located pens at three key note-making points around the house: clipped onto the calendar; by the phone; and in the travel wallet. According to the System, these pens should only ever be removed from their posts to be used for, respectively, noting events on the calendar, taking down phone messages and filling in travel-related documents. My husband is quite strict in his enforcement of this rule, and any pen found being used for a purpose other than that intended is immediately returned to its sentry-post.

And irritating though it is to have a writing implement removed mid-word, I simply do not seem to feel the loss as keenly as does my son. For this I have my prefrontal cortex to thank. A mere smudge of brain cells at birth, it takes twenty-odd years or more to reach its full stature as the sergeant major of the adult brain. One of the many jobs of the prefrontal cortex is to regulate the emotional responses of less civilised brain regions, which is why it's such a useful thing to have. While earning my PhD, I studied a man who had damaged part of his prefrontal cortex in a car accident. Because he had a little problem with his temper (he liked to let a blunt instrument do his arguing for him), he had been removed to a high-security psychiatric hospital for the safety of all. I made the mistake of reading his case-notes just before meeting him and I felt deeply nervous as to how the two of us would hit it off. Unfortunately, when I am anxious my palms become unpleasantly sweaty. As I began to shake hands with the patient, he rapidly withdrew his own with an expression of the utmost disgust, and ostentatiously wiped it on his trousers.

'Christ!' he remarked to my supervisor, who was relishing every moment. 'It's like shaking hands with a wet haddock.'

Had his prefrontal cortex been intact and doing its job, I have no doubt that he would have kept this observation to himself.

There is little doubt that, compared with the toddler or the uninhibited brain-damaged patient, we display a truly authoritative control of our emotions. Nonetheless, it is also the case that our emotions and moods enjoy an impressive mastery of us. It may seem, as we busily go about our lives – deciding what actions are best taken for the future, casting our beady eye over people and events around us and passing judgment on them, or reflecting on the past – that we are making good use of our uniquely human powers of rationality. However, research suggests that it is often our emotions that are actually wearing the pants. Our emotion's sweaty fingers fiddle with our psychological world at every level: from the seemingly straightforward issue of what we perceive in the world around us, to the rich and complex sense of 'me-ness' in the world within us.

Unlike a cow, say, whose alternatives for action are to munch on this little patch of grass, or that little patch of grass, we humans have some labyrinthine decisions to make in our lives. One of the hottest new topics in psychology is the clout our emotions wield over our choices – even those that we might be tempted to think require impressively intellectual calculations and calibrations. The experiment that sparked off this interest in the power of feelings used a gambling game as a laboratory simulation of the complex and uncertain mix of risks and benefits that our everyday choices bring. The researchers asked volunteers to select cards, over and over, from any of the four decks in front of them.[1] They weren't given much information about the decks, just that some worked out better than others. When they turned over a card they learnt whether they had won or lost points. Two of the decks yielded high point gains but, every so often, very severe point losses. This meant that, overall, these packs were best avoided. The other two packs were actually more beneficial in the long run; they offered less dazzling point wins, but less devastating point losses. While the volunteers played the game, the researchers monitored their emotional responses. They did this by measuring their skin conductance response – the polite way of referring to how much someone is sweating. (Skin conductance equipment measures the electrical conductivity of skin, which is affected by the salt in sweat.)

The pattern of winning and losing was too complicated for the volunteers to calculate which decks were the best. Yet by the end of the experiment, nearly all of the volunteers were choosing from the winning packs. They had developed hunches about which decks to avoid. This isn't particularly remarkable in itself, but what was rather eerie was that the volunteers' sweaty fingers seemed to work out which decks to avoid before the volunteers themselves did. In the pre-hunch stage, while the volunteers were still choosing cards haphazardly, their skin conductance responses would shoot up just before they chose a card from a losing deck. Only *after* the volunteers started showing these warning emotional jolts did they develop their gut feeling that they should avoid those decks.

The authority that these gut feelings have over our behaviour became clear when the researchers gave the same gambling game to a patient with damage to part of the prefrontal cortex (the ventro-medial prefrontal lobe). This man, known as EVR, had been a happy and successful businessman, husband and father until a brain tumour developed in part of his prefrontal cortex and had to be removed. Soon after, EVR's professional and personal life went to rack and ruin because of an extraordinary inability to make decisions.[2] The simplest purchases – which razor to buy? what brand of shampoo? – required exhaustive comparisons of price and quality. And you could faint from hunger waiting for him to decide at which restaurant to eat. He would begin with an extensive discussion of each restaurant's seating plan, details of its menu, its atmosphere and its management. Then the field work would begin, in the form of drive-by inspections to see how busy each restaurant was. Yet even after all this research, EVR still found it impossible to choose. EVR's pathological vacillation was so time-consuming that it placed a terminal strain on both his marriage and his employment. And when he did manage to make decisions, they were generally bad ones. Despite numerous warnings from others that he was making a terrible mistake, this once shrewd businessman invested all his savings in a home-building business with a partner of dubious commercial and moral credentials, and went bankrupt.

What was so odd about EVR's condition – and what made it so hard to understand why his post-surgery life was so disastrous – was that his intellect was completely unaffected by his brain injury. The researchers studying him chatted with him for hours about current affairs, politics and ethics, and were unfailingly impressed with his intelligence and knowledge. They quizzed him too on hypothetical social dilemmas, asking him what a person could and should do in tricky social situations. EVR had no trouble in coming up with a whole range of sensible solutions to these problems even though – as he himself cheerfully admitted – he wouldn't have a clue what to decide to do if he ended up in those situations himself.[3]

In fact, it was partly this strange unconcern about his problems that triggered the researchers' suspicions that EVR's failing might be an emotional one. Nothing seemed to touch him emotionally, and this was confirmed by an experiment showing that EVR (and other patients like him) didn't show normal skin conductance increases to emotionally charged pictures (such as scenes of mayhem, mutilation and nudity).[4] Could it be that this emotional lack was behind EVR's debilitating incapacity to make decisions? The researchers investigated this idea using their gambling game, monitoring the skin conductance responses of EVR and other similar patients while they played. In the game, as in life, the patients made poor decisions, never learning to avoid the 'bad' decks. This was despite the fact that half of the patients even came to realise that the high-risk decks they were going for were bad news.[5]

Why couldn't the patients 'solve' the gambling task? Unlike the non-brain-damaged volunteers – who let off an emotional skin-conductance shudder right before choosing from a bad deck, even before they consciously began to suspect that those decks should be avoided – the patients showed no signs of building up this sort of emotional knowledge. The conclusion it is most tempting to draw is that these emotional tags (or somatic markers, as the researchers called them) guide our decision-making. Without these emotional tags, even the most encyclopedic knowledge or powerful intellect cannot help us to pluck a bottle of shampoo off the supermarket shelf.

EVR's chaotically indecisive life vividly demonstrates how disabling it is for us not to have our emotions available as input while we are weighing up our options. Yet using emotions as information brings its own peril – the danger of mistaking the cause of those emotions. If we misattribute our emotion to the wrong source – thinking it stems from some origin other than the one that is actually causing our surge of feeling – this error can be 'carried forward' to our judgments and decisions. Research suggests that this may happen rather more often than we realise.

The problem is that our bodies seem to produce a 'one size fits all' emotional response. For a long time some psychologists had trouble accepting the idea that our hearts thump in pretty much the same way regardless of whether we're in an exam, have just won the lottery or are running for a bus.[6] These die-hard psychologists went to extraordinarily elaborate lengths in their attempts to show that the body responds differently to different emotions. And they spared no amount of emotional trauma in their volunteers along the way. (This was before the concept of 'research ethics', way back in the golden era of psychology when you could hurl an unsuspecting volunteer into the throes of a powerfully distressing emotion and then all have a laugh about it afterwards.) For example, a researcher with the suitably ominous name of Ax asked volunteers to lie down on a medical bed.[7] He then attached them to a complicated tangle of electrodes and wires, and told them to relax. Once they were nice and comfy, unexpectedly, they began to feel electric shocks in their little finger. When they commented on this to the experimenter, he feigned surprise and twiddled a few knobs. Moments later, sparks began to fly across the wires and the experimenter, lab-coat flying with panic, exclaimed that there was a dangerous high voltage short circuit. The volunteer lay awaiting fatal electrocution for about five minutes while the experimenter flapped about creating 'an atmosphere of alarm and confusion', until he finally declared the short circuit repaired and the danger over.

There was no doubt that Ax's volunteers were genuinely scared. One volunteer remarked afterwards, 'Well, everybody has to go some time. I thought this might be my time.' Another prayed to God to be spared death. Yet despite the admirable success of Ax and others in inducing gut-wrenching emotions in their volunteers, it was all in vain. They failed to discover any interesting differences between the physiology of the volunteer trembling with terror and wondering whether his will is in order, and the volunteer about to, say, keel over dead from rage. It is the thoughts that go alongside your emotional arousal that enable you to distinguish between one emotion and another. There's no great mystery to human emotions. All you need to know is one simple equation:[8]

EMOTION = AROUSAL + EMOTIONAL THOUGHTS

Because the arousal is the same whatever the emotion – it varies only in intensity – your brain has the job of matching the arousal with the right thoughts. In fact, when it comes to emotions, your brain is a bit like a laundry assistant matching socks in a hurry before his tea break. When you have two socks that are bright blue with a cartoon dog on them, there's no trouble matching them together. (My brain had little difficulty pairing finding myself confined in a small room with a dangerously uninhibited frontal lobe patient with my sweaty palms.) But when it comes to pairing up all those workaday socks that are only slightly different lengths, styles and hues of black, things get a bit trickier. And your brain isn't all that careful. In lieu of a perfect match, it's happy to snatch up any old black sock that looks about right. The consequence of this is that you attribute your arousal to the wrong thing.

In one such experiment, researchers asked three groups of men to ride an exercise bike for long enough to build up a decent sheen of sweat.[9] They were then given the arduous task of watching an erotic film, and reporting their level of sexual arousal. The first group of men watched and rated the film for its sexually invigorating nature long after they'd recovered from the exercise. Their brains didn't have any problems because there were only two socks to match: the arousal from looking at naked women, and thoughts about the naked women. The second group of men viewed the film straight after exercising. Their brains weren't fooled either. They easily matched the extra arousal with the exercise, and the arousal from the naked women with the thoughts about the naked women. But the last group saw the film a little while after the exercise. By this time, although the men were still physically aroused from the cycling, they weren't aware of it. They had, as it were, lost a sock. This meant that they tidily paired up the arousal from the film and the arousal from the exercise bike with their thoughts about the film. As a result, they rated themselves as significantly more excited by the film than did the other two groups of men. Their emotional brains misled them about how erotic they had found the film. (You might want to bear this experiment in mind next time someone starts flirting with you at the water cooler in the gym: they may have read this book.)

In fact, our emotional brains leave a whole variety of judgments vulnerable to the influence of our moods. When you are walking on the sunny side of the street, your worries really do seem to be left behind on the doorstep. Life seems more satisfying, the grim reaper seems less industrious, politicians even seem less offensive when you are in a cheerful frame of mind.[10] And it can be a remarkably trivial event that tints our spectacles in this rosy fashion. In one classic experiment, a researcher lurking in a shopping mall posed as a company representative and offered some customers (but not others) a small gift, to 'introduce them to the company's products'.[11] Then a second researcher standing a short distance away asked them (as part of a 'customer survey') to rate the performance of their cars and televisions. The free gift was about as desirable as the contents of a mid-range Christmas cracker. Nonetheless, it put the customers who received it into a rather jolly mood, compared with the others. These happy customers – clutching their newly acquired nail-clippers – rated their cars and TVs significantly more positively than did the customers without gifts. In another well-known experiment, when researchers rang students on either a sunny or a rainy day, and asked them about their current happiness and their satisfaction with life in general, the students contacted during fine weather were in better moods than the students contacted while it was raining.[12] In line with what we've already learnt, their weather-influenced mood affected the students' satisfaction with their lives: students contacted on sunny days were more satisfied with their lives.

Even our perception of something as physically grounded as pain can be swayed by lightness of heart, and not simply because we are distracted from our physical symptoms. I must confess that, pregnant for the second time and reading a list of pain-management techniques for labour, I scoffed loud and hard at the suggestion that expectant parents keep the birthing room sweetened with the smell of aromatherapy oils. Yet research suggests that, even when we are completely focused on our bodily discomfort, the lifting of mood that comes from a pleasant olfactory environment can reduce suffering. Volunteers were asked to rate the intensity and unpleasantness of heat pain applied to their arm.[13] At the same time, their nasal region was suffused with either a pleasant or an unpleasant smell. The volunteers' ratings of the intensity of the pain weren't much affected by whether they were inhaling a delicious scent or a foul stench. However, their mood was very sensitive to the prevailing aroma. With spirits lifted by fragrant wafts, the volunteers found the pain significantly less unpleasant, compared with their experience when the odour was unpleasant. (Despite the findings of this experiment, I have yet to hear a new mother utter the words, 'Yes, labour was pretty tough … until Darren fired up the aromatherapy burner, that is.')

Gloom has just the opposite effect on our view of the world around us. Life seems more hazardous, relationship conflicts seem more of our own doing, and racial minorities seem less likeable when we are in a bad mood.[14] Psychologists are still squabbling over exactly how and when moods influence our judgments.[15] However, it looks as though at least some of the time our moods mislead us in the same way that misattributed arousal can. If we haven't registered why we're in a particular mood, then sometimes we erroneously use that mood to inform our opinions about things. In the experiment in which students were asked about their lives over the phone, on either sunny or rainy days, some students were asked casually at the start of the interview, 'By the way, how's the weather down there?' These students didn't let their present mood colour or confuse their judgments when it came to their feelings about their life satisfaction. Reminded by the telephone surveyor that their mood was probably due to the weather, these students successfully and appropriately must have dismissed their spirits as irrelevant to the question in hand.

It is certainly disquieting that our emotions and moods have such an impact on our judgments. However, as the weather-sensitive telephone survey experiment shows, at least we can sometimes protect ourselves from the undulations of our humour, so long as we are aware of being off our usual emotional keel. Yet emotion's meddlesome fingers can act more surreptitiously still, striking so early on in the process of interpreting what is around us that there is no hope of resistance. For emotions enjoy the dangerous ability to affect what we experience, not just how we interpret it. To see how even mildly experienced emotions influence perception, researchers manipulated people's mood using happy or sad music and films.[16] Then the volunteers watched two movies of the face of an actor. In one movie, the actor's beaming smile gradually faded until his expression was neutral. In the other movie, it was a sad pout that disappeared into neutrality, frame by frame. The task of the volunteer was to stop the movie at the point they felt that the person they were watching was no longer happy (or sad). The volunteer's artificially induced mood had a remarkable effect on their perception of the actor's facial expression: cheerful volunteers saw a smile lingering for longer than they did the frown. To the eyes of the gloomy volunteers, however, it was the mopey face that reflected their own state of mind that made the most protracted departure from the actor's face. The world may not really be smiling with you when you smile; it might just look that way thanks to the misleading gloss applied by the emotional brain. Our visual experiences are so compelling, so real and seemingly objective that it is hard to acknowledge the furtive role played by the brain in creating what we see. Could it really be that the unpleasant look that you saw, plain as day, pass over your spouse's face has more to do with your own frazzled mood than that fleeting arrangement of her facial features? It is all but impossible to believe, but the research suggests that her protestation of innocence may actually be genuine.

Our emotional feelings towards other people can also inspire the mind's eye to engage its artistic license liberally. There is empirical proof that we can be almost literally blinded (or at least seriously visually impaired) by love or hatred; or rather – in the low-key fashion of the ethically guided modern laboratory experiment – by liking or disliking. To inspire such sentiments in unsuspecting volunteers, a stooge was trained to behave in either an exceptionally likeable or objectionable fashion.[17] For some volunteers, the charming stooge (supposedly another volunteer in the experiment) sported a sweatshirt from the real volunteer's own university. When her tardiness was commented on by the experimenter, she was winningly apologetic, and made amends by generously proffering cookies all round. In the other scenario, the stooge advertised on her clothing her allegiance to a rival university. In response to the experimenter's mild remark about her late arrival, she snapped irritably words to the effect that if they could just cut the chat then they could all get on with it. Then, helping herself (and herself alone) to cookies, the stooge rammed in the earphones of her walkman and – in an act that guaranteed rousing feelings of enmity – cranked up the volume to a level audible to all.

The volunteers were then assigned to be either the player or observer of a very simple computerised tennis game. By means of one of those rigged draws at which social psychologists are so proficient, the stooge was deputed to play the tennis game against the computer. The true volunteer was chosen to be the observer. Their task was to watch the game in an adjacent cubicle, and for every volley (a flash of light appearing on the screen) to indicate whether it fell in or out of bounds. Crucially, the volunteer was told that their calls as linesman would have no effect whatsoever on the game. They were merely providing the experimenter with information about the game's clarity. The computer itself could of course determine whether the flash of light fell in or out of bounds, and points would be won or lost according to this more authoritative source. So, to belabour the point, the volunteers knew that they had no influence on the game, and that there was no purpose to be served – either benevolent or malevolent, depending on their feelings towards the stooge playing the game – by reporting untruthfully whether or not balls fell in or outside the boundary line.

Yet remarkably, the volunteers' sentiments towards the stooge still biased what they actually saw. When a ball hit by the stooge fell just a few pixels within the line, volunteers still seething from her incivilities were more likely to mistakenly call it out. Balls that were actually out, but supposedly hit by the stooge's computerised opponent, these volunteers were more likely to call as in. Equally partisan, and exactly opposite, were the perceptions of those who felt warmly towards the amiable stooge. Their errors in calling balls that were just in or out favoured the stooge over her computerised adversary. There was presumably no agenda being served, either consciously or unconsciously, by the volunteer's mistakes, since they were well aware that they were incapable of affecting the outcome of the game. Yet their attitude towards the stooge powerfully influenced what they actually saw, at the most basic level.

The emotional brain does not just tinker with our impression of the here and now, as we have already seen from the previous chapter. A habitually over-cheerful mental outlook goes hand-in-hand with unrealistically optimistic predictions about the future. (Conversely, those of us who are sadder but wiser seem to be more realistic about what is likely to lie ahead.) Nor does the past lie safely untouched by the emotional brain's reparative activities. Using a strategy known as the fading affect bias, the brain tampers with our memory of events we have already experienced.[18] History is rewritten such that the distressing emotions we experienced when things went wrong are looked back on as having been less and less intense, as time goes by. In contrast, the brain's biographer does its best to lovingly nurture and sustain the vigour of memories of past joys. This differential treatment of the past leaves us susceptible to believing that our past was happier that it truly was.

At this point you might be wondering whether the humble cow, unperturbably munching grass, might not have a more accurate view of her world than we do of ours. Our decisions, opinions, perception and memory can all be set adrift by our emotional undercurrents – often without our even noticing that our anchor has slipped. Perhaps more surprising still, though, is the role that these squeakings and creakings of the emotional brain in action play in generating our sense of self. For as we will learn, they seem to be what generate our very sense of existence, or *being*.

Think back to the most nerve-wracking experience of your life. Did you feel as if you weren't actually there? It's very likely that you felt an eerie detachment from yourself, as if some sort of 'out-of-body you' were dispassionately observing you. Perhaps most curious of all is that, rather than experiencing the shakes and quakes merited by the situation, you felt peculiarly emotionless.

My own traumatic experience of this sort occurred in the unlikely venue of a science museum. I was newly employed as an 'Explainer', a lone psychologist amid a cluster of biochemists. While the biochemists admired the genetic material they had cleverly unleashed from onion cells – an activity deemed suitable for children aged five and up – I gazed bewildered at my *soupe d'oignon*, and not a chromosome in sight. These über-Explainers pipetted, centrifuged and chromatographed their way through the training with ease, while I knocked over the test tubes of myself and others, and wished that I had been born with hands rather than paws.

By the day of my first workshop my well-founded anxieties about my competence were alleviated only by the knowledge that I would be joined by one of the superbly competent Explainers. I anticipated expertly assisting in the distribution of lab-coats and then allowing the biochemist to pull her weight by running the workshop. However, I turned out to be a superior Explainer to her in one important respect. I remembered to attend the workshop.

I was terrified. My mission was to guide twelve prepubescents through the Frankensteinian mutation of *E. coli* bacteria. The children were beginning to fidget: some choosing to play with the alarmingly expensive scientific equipment; others preferring to jiggle the flimsy petri dishes containing potentially lethal bacteria. It was at that moment that my brain did a runner. My 'me', so to speak, slipped out of my body and watched impassively as Cordelia Fine ran a science workshop. Thanks to my brain, I was able to do a much better job than if I had remained in there, gripped in the clutch of terror. The *E. coli* may have remained unmutated – and the children possibly wondered what all that scientific equipment was actually *for* – but there were no fatalities or lawsuits. (Despite this, shortly after this incident it was suggested to me that I might prefer to never Explain anything in the museum ever again.)

What I was experiencing in those few hours of intense anxiety was what psychologists call depersonalisation. It's an ace your brain keeps up its sleeve for when the chips are down. You feel detached from your thoughts, feelings and body, and the world may seem dreamy and unreal. Once the coast is clear your brain brings you back again, and the world is real once more.

What is your brain up to during depersonalisation episodes? Thanks to those pesky research ethics that prioritise bothersome issues such as people's welfare and rights over furtherance of scientific knowledge, psychologists can't simply recruit a handful of generous volunteers, throw them into a terrifying situation and then take a few measurements. Instead, they have been studying people with a psychiatric condition called depersonalisation disorder that leaves them in an almost constant state of out-of-bodyness.[19] Like the depersonalisation you may have experienced yourself, it is often set off by intensely anxious episodes. This is almost certainly no coincidence. Depersonalisation seems to be the emotional brain's emergency response to stress and anxiety. In the face of severe threat, your brain throws up its hands in defeat and switches off the emotions at the mains. This prevents you from becoming overwhelmed with anxiety, which could be literally fatal in a dangerous situation.

But if the emotions are off, they're off. There aren't separate stopcocks for 'crazy psychologist telling me I'm about to be electrocuted to death' emotions and 'damn, I've got a parking ticket' emotions. So if the theory about depersonalisation is right, patients should be unemotional about everything. Sure enough, when psychologists showed depersonalisation disorder patients nasty pictures, they didn't show the normal leap in skin conductance response.[20] The patients just weren't emotionally aroused by the unpleasant pictures in the way people usually are.

The same researchers then looked directly into the brains of

the depersonalisation patients using functional magnetic reso-
nance imaging, the whizz-bang imaging technology that measures
brain activity.[21] They wanted to see how the patients' brains
responded to disgusting things. Going round to the patients'
houses and performing an enema on the kitchen table wasn't on
the cards (those research ethics committees again), so it was back
to the pictures. Normally, a part of the brain called the insula
goes wild when you see disgusting things. It's the part of your
brain that stays forever eight years old. But the insulas of the
depersonalisation patients actually responded *less* to disgusting
pictures than they did to boring pictures. What *was* getting overly
excited, however, was our old friend, the prefrontal cortex.

Because the prefrontal cortex is in charge of keeping our emotions in check, there is a huge amount of communication
between the prefrontal cortex and areas of the brain like the
insula that respond to emotional stimuli. This is why it was so
interesting that the sergeant major of the brain was over-active in
the patients with depersonalisation disorder when they looked
at disgusting pictures in the brain imaging study. Unlike my
charming patient with the damaged prefrontal cortex, whose
emotions were allowed to run wild and free, the prefrontal
cortices of the depersonalisation disorder patients seemed to be
holding the emotions on too tight a rein. It looked as if, at the
merest glimpse of something a little juicy, the prefrontal cortex
started shooting commands down to the insula, warning it to
keep its mouth shut. This excessive nannying by your prefrontal
cortex may be how your emotional brain is able to shut itself off
during depersonalisation episodes.

It might seem rather appealing, the idea of remaining so untouched by the emotional flotsam of life. One imagines depersonalisation patients greeting an astronomical phone bill with a lackadaisical shrug, a leaking roof with a careless laugh. But in fact depersonalisation is an extremely unpleasant state to be in for any length of time. Self-injury and self-mutilation aren't uncommon in depersonalisation patients, perhaps as an attempt to just feel *something*. Life is flat and disturbingly unreal:[22]

> Music usually moves me, but now it might as well be someone mincing potatoes … I seem to be walking about in a world I recognise but don't feel … It's the terrible isolation from the rest of the world that frightens me. It's having no contact with people or my husband. I talk to them and see them, but I don't feel they are really here.

As one patient put it, 'I would rather be dead than continue living like this. It is like the living dead.' That's the problem with depersonalisation. You no longer feel as if you're experiencing life:

> It is as if the real me is taken out and put on a shelf or stored somewhere inside of me. Whatever makes me me is not there.

> I feel as though I'm not alive – as though my body is an empty, lifeless shell.

This is what suggests that it is our emotional brain that gifts us with our sense of self. It is our feelings, no matter how trivial, that let us know we are alive.[23] We see the toilet seat left up *again*, and, while we writhe in fury, the brain chuckles, 'Yep, still here.' According to this line of argument, if the emotions were shut off tight enough a person might actually begin to believe that they no longer exist ...

> One day I went out for a walk, right round town and ended up at my mother-in-law's and said to her, 'I'm dead' and started stabbing at my arm to try and get some blood out. It wouldn't bleed so I was saying 'Look, I must be dead – there's no blood.'[24]

This man wasn't mucking around trying to embarrass his mother-in-law in front of her friends from the tennis club. He genuinely believed himself to be dead. In the same way, another patient, a young woman, expressed guilt about drawing social security payments. She was worried that, being dead, she wasn't really eligible for her benefits. These patients suffer from the Cotard delusion, which some researchers think might be the result of a brain being even more excessive in its depersonalisation strategy. While to the depersonalisation patient the world seems distant or unreal, the Cotard patient may deny that the world even exists. While the depersonalisation disorder patient may feel as if their body no longer belongs to them, the Cotard patient may claim that parts of their body have rotted away altogether. And while the depersonalisation disorder patient may feel *as if* they were dead, the Cotard patient may actually believe it.

In these extreme cases of the Cotard delusion, so detached do patients feel from their feelings, thoughts, body and the world that nothing can persuade them that they are alive. One of the first Cotard patients to be reported, described by a psychiatrist in the 19th century, insisted upon being laid out on a shroud. She then began to fuss over the inadequate appearance of the linen, provoking the psychiatrist to complain irritably that 'even in death she cannot abstain from her female habit of beautifying herself …'. The feeling of non-existence is inescapably compelling. Psychologists asked the young female Cotard patient with concerns about her eligibility for social security how she could feel heat and cold, feel her heart beat, feel when her bladder was full yet, despite this, nonetheless claim to be dead. The young woman cleverly replied that since she had these feelings despite being dead, they clearly could not be taken as good evidence that she was alive – a rebuttal that would possibly have stymied Descartes himself.

In fact, when Descartes famously wrote 'cogito, ergo sum', 'cogito' referred not just to thinking, but to a rich variety of experiences, including emotions. Depersonalisation suggests that when the brain turns down the volume on the emotions, your sense of self begins to slip away.

The balance that the sergeant major of the emotional brain has to achieve is a delicate one. Too much emotion and we wind up bawling over a ballpoint pen that someone has taken from us, detained in a secure psychiatric hospital, or paralysed with terror in the face of a few schoolchildren and several million *E. coli* bacteria. Yet if the emotional brain becomes too stingy with the emotions, the consequences can be no less devastating. As the chronically indecisive patient EVR demonstrates, remove the ability to use emotions as information and the simplest decision becomes irredeemably perplexing. Dampen down the emotions too much and we begin to lose grasp of our precious sense of self. And even when the sergeant major gets the balance about right, we are left mildly deluded about our past, present and future. Emotional aftermath from incidental circumstances – the gift of a cheap freebie, a spot of rain, the agitation of light exercise, a pungent air freshener – can all colour our seemingly dispassionate views. Your brain has its sweaty fingers in all the pies, from the shampoo you try to the smiles you spy. Considering how much backstairs influence it has in constructing your outer and inner worlds, better hope that your emotional brain is doing a reasonable job.

CHAPTER 3

The Immoral Brain

The terrible toddler within

The moral world of my two-year-old son is simple; it is grounded in emotions as raw as they are powerful.

'*Isaac's* turn!' he thunders at the child who has just climbed into the playground swing.

'That's *mine!*' he admonishes the baby, snatching the toy away.

'Don't *want* it!' is his verdict on the nappy I am struggling to put on him, careless as he is to the potentially disastrous consequences for the well-being of the sofa.

'*Isaac* do it!' he wails in agonies of envy at the sight of his father chopping onions with a very sharp knife.

There is no evidence in his demeanour of internal struggles over complex issues of reciprocity, possession, duty or prudence. The path of righteousness is plain as day – it corresponds exactly to what my son wants.

Nor does he concern himself with the subtle complexities of people's circumstances before passing judgment on their transgressions.

'Naughty Greta!' he pronounces as his three-year-old friend throws her dinner across the room.

Greta's mother carefully explains to my son that Greta herself is not naughty, but – being tired, hungry and overexcited – yes, Greta did do a naughty thing. My son, however, clearly has no time for the modern practice of labelling the behaviour, not the child. 'Naughty Greta', he insists. Then, after a thoughtful pause, 'Naughty Greta, naughty Greta, naughty Greta!' Indeed, to re-inforce his point that no allowances will be made for substandard behaviour at the dinner table, he says nothing else but this for the rest of our visit.

I anticipate, of course, that – learning from his parents' impeccable example and instruction – my son will outgrow his primitive and solipsistic moral sense. Or at least learn to conceal it better. For scratch the surface of the moral judgments of mature adulthood, and visceral iniquities worthy of the passionate toddler can be plainly seen. Carelessly unattuned to the circum-stances of others, we can be as quick to conclude 'naughty Greta' as any stripling magistrate. And yet when the tables are turned and our own situation makes it hard to do the right thing, it turns out that our conduct is as capricious as that of any 'terrible' two-year-old.

It may not be quite as transparent in adults as it is in young child-ren, but nonetheless our emotions play an important, if furtive, role in our moral condemnations and approbations. According to one recent hypothesis, these seemingly lofty judgments usually stem from instant gut feelings or 'moral intuitions'.[1] As we ponder a morally charged situation we feel a primitive flash of emotion, which is all we need in order to pass our judgment. However, as it's a shame to leave resting idle those parts of our brain that help to distinguish us from apes and toddlers, we then invent reasons to explain and justify our view. (And, as you will see in 'The Pigheaded Brain', the brain is disturbingly adept at supplying a conveniently biased array of evidence and arguments to bolster its opinions.) This gives us the satisfying though often illusory impression that our morals are based on reasoned and logical thought, rather than cartoon-esque reflexes such as 'yuk!', 'ouch!' or 'tsk!'. Thanks to the emotional brain's clever deception, it normally seems – both to ourselves and others – that we engaged in our skilful cogitations before, rather than after, forming our moral verdict. Yet when there are no good reasons around to justify our knee-jerk responses, the fact that we are grasping at non-existent straws of rational thought in the moralising process becomes embarrassingly apparent.

For example, researchers asked some university students to justify their moral condemnation of (I shall put this as delicately as I am able) a man self-pleasuring with the willing assistance of a dog.[2] According to the Western framework of morality which can be summed up crudely as 'anything goes, so long as nobody gets hurt', there is nothing morally wrong with this mutually enjoyable interaction between a man and his best friend, icky though it is to contemplate. That's why many of the students had a hard time rationalising their reflexive 'yuk' responses and, as the researchers put it, became 'morally dumbfounded'. 'Well, I just, I don't know, I don't think that's, I guess [long pause], I don't really [laughter] think of these things much, so I don't really know but, I don't know, I just [long pause], um …' was one student's inarticulate attempt to explain her censure of the man-with-dog scenario, for example. Moral intuitions based on unthinking emotions may not always serve us too well, then, if our aim is a coherent and consistent moral sense. Our own discomfort or disgust may not always be compatible with the moral framework to which we claim to subscribe.

Emotions muck up our attempts to be fair and just in another way too. As we saw in the last chapter, feelings triggered by one event can be wrongly incorporated into the processes we use to pass judgment on other matters. (Remember the shoppers who rated their cars and televisions more highly because they were in a good mood from receiving a free gift?) Unfortunately, this interfering effect of emotions can also wreak havoc on our moral judgments, which are susceptible to exactly the same sort of bias. In a demonstration of the distorting effects of anger, for example, researchers set one group of volunteers boiling with rage by showing them a video in which they witnessed the brutal beating of a teenager.[3] A second group of volunteers watched instead a film of colourful shapes frolicking innocuously across the screen. Then, in a supposedly unrelated experiment, all the volunteers were asked to pass judgment on a series of negligence cases. They were asked, for example, about a construction site manager who failed to check the temporary boards covering the sidewalk. To what extent was he to blame for the broken ankle and collarbone of a passer-by who tripped on a gap in those boards? How much compensation should he pay the injured party for their pain and suffering? Volunteers still seething over the injustice they had watched on the video committed their own injustice in turn on the negligence defendants. These angry people were harsher in their recriminations of those who had neglected their duties, and were more heavy-handed in their declarations of what they would consider to be their just deserts, compared with the volunteers who weren't experiencing carryover rage.

And this is not the only way that being hot-headed makes us wrong-headed. Being blinded by rage does nothing for our ability to perceive the subtle nuances of moral dilemmas. In some of the negligence cases read by both the angry and the calm volunteers, the culprits acted entirely of their own free will (for example, a second-hand car-dealer who knowingly sold a lemon to an unsuspecting customer). However, in other cases, complicating factors such as a lack of training or coercion by superiors were incorporated into the scenarios. The site manager, for example, had been given no instructions about how to check the safety of the site before leaving. What is more, his shift was over for the day and he knew he would be paid no overtime for checking the boards, because the job was losing money. The dispassionate volunteers were sensitive to this, recognising that these mitigating circumstances made the defendants deserve less punishment. The angry volunteers, in contrast, negligently ignored these niceties as they clumsily attempted to balance the scales of retributive justice.

The moral fog that comes from being in a state of vexation is not inevitable, however. Some of the angry volunteers, before passing judgment, were told that they would later be questioned by a post-doctoral researcher about the reasons behind their apportioning of blame. These volunteers, knowing that they would have to justify their finger pointing, behaved more like the unemotional volunteers when they set penalties for the wrong-doers. It is reassuring, I suppose, that we are able to overcome the distorting effects of our emotional state when we know we are to be held accountable. On the other hand, how dispiriting that we only take the trouble to keep our own moods out of the moral equation when we know that we may be pulled up for not doing so.

Our moral judgments are also dangerously polluted by a deep-rooted need to believe in a just world.[4] All of us have of course outgrown the fairy-tale notion that virtue is always rewarded and bad guys get their comeuppance. (Down here on earth, at least. Plenty of adults cling to the hope that justice will be served in the afterlife: the person of honour will be waved through the pearly gates; the scoundrel will come back as a cockroach.) Ask us outright, and we will tut and sigh at the undeserved misfortunes of the world's many innocent victims. And yet, presented with such unfortunates, our feelings towards them can belie our lofty principles.[5] When our eldest son was still a baby (and, of course, the centre of our world) we took him out for a stroll and bumped into a neighbour, a grandmother of three. It was the tenth birthday of one of her granddaughters – or would have been, had the little girl not died of leukaemia three years before. Our neighbour told us the harrowing details of her granddaughter's physical decline, her painful cancer treatments, and the hopeless despair of the last few months before she died. I am not proud of this, but all through the telling of this unbearably sad story, frantic accusations against the bereaved mother kept hurling themselves, unbidden, into my consciousness: 'she can't have breastfed', 'I'll bet she fed her junk food', even, 'she let her sit too close to the television'. At one level I knew that these thoughts were grossly unwarranted and completely irrational. Yet still they came. The ominous message of this poor woman's loss – 'it could be your child' – was too distressing to contemplate. My immoral brain's despicable and shameful strategy for coping with this threat was to blame the mother. It was her fault, she brought it upon herself, she failed in her maternal duties ... the unvoiced reassurance of these vilifications is ultimately, of course, 'I needn't worry. It won't happen to me.'

Although such denial is not normally quite so transparent, I am not alone in this cowardly practice. The myriad injustices of the world are simply too much for our delicate psyches. Faced with some wretched prey of fate, we struggle against the conclusion that life is savagely, mercilessly unfair. If it is impossible, too difficult or too much trouble to fight for a victim's wrong to be righted, to recompense them for their suffering or to relieve them of their burden, then we succumb to another, easier strategy. We persuade ourselves that they have brought their misfortune onto themselves. So strong is our need to believe in a just world (since otherwise we, too – through no fault of our own – might lose our job, our home, our health, our sanity, our child), that we yield to the more comfortable delusion that bad things happen to bad people.

Evidence of our stubborn belief in a just world comes in part from a series of experiments which cleverly expose how our feelings towards people alter, for the worse, when we are forced to watch them suffer. In this devious experimental set-up, several volunteers are ushered into an auditorium. They are told that

they will watch on CCTV a fellow volunteer in a learning experiment. Their task is to rate her behavioural cues. The researcher,
Dr Stewart, arrives and leads her experimentee from the room. As
they make their way out, Dr Stewart comments that this session's
learning experiment will involve strong electric shocks as punishment for errors on the learning task. The unfortunate student is
led from the room like a lamb to the slaughter, and shortly afterwards the observers see on the TV screen the volunteer being
attached to the electrodes. By way of helping her to learn pairs of
words she is shocked, painfully, every time she makes a mistake.

As you have guessed already, the unlucky volunteer is in fact
a stooge; and the CCTV image of the learning experiment is a
previously recorded tape. The researchers are not really interested
in the learner's behavioural cues at all. That's simply a cover story
both to explain why the observers have to watch someone in pain,
and to make the observers somewhat complicit in the ethically
dubious research. Before the observers watch the tape, the experimenter manipulates what they think will happen to the victim
after the first round of electric shocks. For example, the observers
might be told that the victim will go on to receive (in increasingly
tolerable scenarios), nothing, a modest payment, or a generous
payment for her participation in the experiment. But in a different, even more unpleasant version of the ruse, the observers
might be told that the poor victim will receive yet more shocks
in a second stage of the learning experiment. And in the 'martyr'
script of the cover story, the observers learn that the shocked student will be suffering so that they might gain. On hearing that she
is going to be electrocuted, the stooge nervously proclaims that

she is terrified by the idea, and could she please withdraw from the experiment. But the steely Dr Stewart admonishes her, pointing out that, if she backs out, all the students who are supposed to be observing her won't receive their reward for taking part in the experiment. Reluctantly, the martyred victim agrees to carry on for the sake of the observers.

After watching the film of the learning experiment (an obviously distressing experience for those looking on, who jerk in sympathy with the writhings of the stooge), the observers are asked to rate the victim's personality. They have all seen exactly the same tape of her participating in the learning experiment. Yet their perception of what kind of person she is turns out to be surprisingly sensitive to what they think will happen to her next. Remarkably – and horribly – the less monetary compensation the observers think that the victim will receive for her suffering (in other words, the more unfair the experiment), the more they dislike her. Disparaged even more is the woman whom people think will go on to suffer more with a further bout of electric shocks. And what of the martyr, who selflessly sacrificed herself in order to benefit others? She, I am afraid to say, is the most despised of all.

The conclusion of this research – that a person's misfortune is compounded by the commensurately undeserved censure they attract – is chilling indeed. Nor do we have to search our souls too deeply to find examples that fit suspiciously well with the belief in a just world hypothesis. Why, after Hurricane Katrina's destruction of New Orleans, were so many unsubstantiated rumours of rape and violence so widely disseminated?[6] Could it be because it is easier to believe that people get what they deserve? Nobody wants to imagine the frail and impoverished stranded in a devastated city – it tugs less on the heartstrings if we suppose those left behind to be rapists and thugs.

The immoral brain does not just serve our craven psychological need to feel that life is fair and secure. It also competently assists in maintaining that all-important sense of moral superiority. As the brain plays amateur psychologist, speculating as to the reasons and explanations behind why people behave as they do, it is careful to apply double standards whenever necessary. We are, for example, quick to call upon people's personalities as a way of explaining their slip-ups. While at first glance this might seem reasonable, now try considering how often – rather than take this broad-brush tack with yourself – you prefer to make specific excuses for your own behaviour when it falls below par. You're never late on your deadlines because you're inconsiderate and disorganised – it's just that other unexpected and pressing matters arose. You're not ratty and rude – only a saint doesn't occasionally snap at their partner after a long and tiring day. And it's not because you're selfish and uncaring that you haven't yet got round to making that charitable donation – you've had a lot of other things on your plate. When your conduct falls short of your intentions, calling upon mitigating circumstances keeps you safe from the uncomfortable conclusion that you might really be incompetent, unkind or uncharitable.

Do we bother to extend to others the same benefit of the doubt? No. When we muse upon shortcomings in our own conduct, it's obvious that our troubling circumstances conspired to hide our true potential, our good character and our virtuous intent. But we are strangely blind to how the subtleties of other people's situations might affect them. Our sensitivity to the context, so sharply tuned when we apply it to ourselves, becomes sloppy and careless when we focus on others. To our neglectful eye, what other people do reflects what kind of person they are; simple as that. We saw in 'The Vain Brain' how students, asked to predict when they would complete an assignment set by the researcher, failed to take into account their past difficulties in finishing work on time.[7] We have a tendency to blame our past failures to meet deadlines on disruption by unexpected and unforeseeable events, a habit that leaves fresh and unsullied our confidence that *this* time – yes! – we will get things done on time. But when we are forecasting task completion dates for other people, bygone failures suddenly seem much more germane. In the same study, volunteers who were given information about another student's previous failures to finish work on time were much more pessimistic in their predictions about when that student would complete the assignment. Indeed, presumably concluding that they must surely be in the presence of a chronic procrastinator, the scathing onlookers actually overestimated how long it would take the person they were judging to get the job done. Our own cargoes are delayed in the choppy seas of circumstance. Other people's ships sail into harbour late because of their shilly-shallying.

It's cheering, in the midst of all this disquieting research about our self-deception and hypocrisy, to learn one positive thing: we are, it seems, good enough to extend to those we love the same forgiving style of explaining behaviour that we use on ourselves. In fact, much of the time we interpret the reasons behind our partner's behaviour even more benignly than we do our own[8] (perhaps because, as one cynical relationship expert put it, 'being involved with a wonderful person is much more flattering than being involved with an inadequate person'[9]). Indeed, this benevolent fog surrounding the whys and wherefores of our partner's actions seems to be an important characteristic of happy relationships. By contrast, couples teetering on the brink of divorce each judge themselves morally superior to their partner, and observe each other's behaviour with the harshest suspicion.[10] Even kind and thoughtful acts are dismissed as unusual aberrations set against a background of inadequacy. Yet even among couples who are reasonably satisfied with the state of their marriages, the softening haze that shrouds our partner's behaviour can be quickly dispersed just when we need it most. Couples interviewed individually about a conflict they had experienced in their marriage furnished the usual self-serving explanations as to why the circumstances of the quarrel justified their own behaviour.[11] As in the school playground, ringing with cries of 'He started it!', although both spouses were describing the same row, almost everyone claimed that it was the other person's fault. As if their life-partner were no more to them than a stranger, they were mostly oblivious to ways in which the particular situation might vindicate their spouse.

Our appraisals of others also fail to take the same generous account of good intentions that we allow ourselves. Researchers asked volunteers to hold their arms in buckets of icy water for charity, and fifty cents was donated by the researcher for every minute the arm was kept submerged.[12] The volunteers were then asked to rate their own altruism. Mopping the icy droplets from their frozen limbs, the volunteers' measure of their virtue was based less on how much they had actually earned for their chosen charity, than on how much they would have liked to help the charity. In other words, they generously judged themselves by what they *wanted* to do, rather than by what they actually did. But while our own philanthropic thoughts are clear as paint to us, the sheer invisibility of other people's intentions make them all too easy to overlook when we form our opinions of their actions. We give others less credit for their good intentions that we give ourselves for ours. Another group of volunteers in the cold water submersion experiment, asked only to look on as others sacrificed themselves for charity, were not interested in mere motives. When asked to rate the altruism of the person they were watching, they were indifferent to the sufferer's virtuous intent. They judged purely by results. And even those of us who are joined together in holy matrimony have a hard time bringing our spouse's commendable motives under the same strong spotlight that our own enjoy. The married couples I described earlier, who were interviewed about past disputes, were four times more likely to call attention to their own laudable intentions than to those of their partners.

Our indulgent self-approbation, together with our belittlingly imprecise estimations of others, leaves pretty well all of us with the pleasant, though misguided, sense of being holier than thou. Yet in truth, the manipulations of social psychologists show that our moral backbone can be snapped like the flimsiest reed. One of psychology's most famous landmarks, the Milgram obedience studies, exposed just how powerful social situations are in controlling our behaviour. In the original Milgram obedience study, forty ordinary and presumably decent men (teachers, engineers and labourers, for example) were recruited to take part in a study of 'memory and learning' at Yale University.[13] The cover story was that, together with another participant, they would be taking the role of either teacher or learner in an experiment designed to look at the effects of punishment on learning. In a rigged random draw, the unsuspecting man was deputed to be the teacher. The other participant – a pleasant-mannered stooge – drew the role of learner.

The level of detail devoted to deceiving the volunteers in this infamous experiment was extraordinary. First, the stooge was strapped into an electric chair (to 'prevent excessive movement', they were told), and electrode paste applied beneath the electrodes that were attached to the learner's wrists (so as to 'avoid blisters and burns'). The real participant, brought into a different room, meanwhile learned that, as the teacher, his job was to deliver increasingly powerful electric shocks whenever the learner made a mistake on a word-pair learning task. The sham electric shock generator (professionally engraved with the words 'Shock Generator, Type ZLB, Dyson Instrument Company, Waltham, Mass. Output 15 Volts–450 Volts') included a panel with 30 switches labelled from 15 to 450 volts, in 15-volt increments. The intensity of the different levels of shock were helpfully described on the control panel. For example, the 15- to 60-volt switches were categorised as 'Slight Shock', while the switches from 375 to

420 volts were labelled 'Danger: Severe Shock'. The final two levels of shock, 435 and 450 volts, were simply and ominously marked 'XXX'. To add a final touch of authenticity to the faux shock generator, at the start of the experiment each teacher was given a 45 volts shock, supposedly from the generator but actually from a battery hidden within it.

The scene set, it was time for the 'learning experiment' to begin. The teacher was told to move the switch up 15 volts every time the learner made a mistake. At 300 volts the learner pounded audibly on the wall of his experimental prison, and made no response to the teacher's question. Generally, the teacher would ask the experimenter what to do at this point, to which the experimenter would reply that he should treat the absence of a response as a wrong answer, and increase the shock level another 15 volts. There was another desperate banging on the wall at 315 volts, and from then on there was nothing but sinister silence from the learner – not even the reassurance of a frenzied hammering. Back on the other side, the teacher participants showed signs of extreme agitation: sweating profusely, trembling, stuttering, biting their lips, groaning, digging fingernails into their flesh. Some men even began to smile and laugh nervously – uncontrollably so, in three cases. Many of the participants questioned the experimenter about whether they should continue, or expressed concern for the damage that they might be doing to the learner. In response to their anxieties, the experimenter politely, but increasingly firmly, responded that they should continue.

What Milgram famously (and repeatedly) found is that about two-thirds of ordinary men (and women) will obediently electrocute a fellow human being, all the way up to a highly dangerous 450 volts, because a scientist in a lab-coat tells them to do so. And nearly 90 per cent of the participants in the original experiment administered at least one more shock after hearing the learner pound on the wall. The experimenter had no special power to enforce his strictures to continue. Nor would the men have been punished in any way for defying the experimenter. Yet despite the clear signs that the learner was suffering against his will, the authority of the situation was too much for most people to withstand. The majority of participants broke the simple moral tenet, learned at mother's knee, not to hurt other people.

The morally stifling effect of being at the bottom of the authority gradient, as it is known, is certainly nothing short of remarkable. The reluctance of a co-pilot to pipe up and challenge his captain's judgment has been estimated to be significant in as many as one in five airline crashes.[14] So powerful are the psychological pressures of a hierarchical environment that a co-pilot may sacrifice himself – as well as passengers and crew – rather than question his superior's authority. On 1 December 1993, Express II Airlines Inc./Northwest Airlink Flight 5719 to Hibbing, Minnesota, descended too steeply, missing the runway altogether. Everyone on board was killed. The cockpit voice recording revealed that the co-pilot knew that the plane was at too high an altitude for the descent. 'Just … you just gonna stay up here as long as you can?' was his single tentative attempt to alert the captain to his error. Even as the plane was brushing the treetops, moments before the crash, the co-pilot was deferentially answering the captain's questions.

In another notorious and sobering experiment showing that

the murmur of internal virtue is easily drowned out by the noisy demands of our circumstances, researchers Darley and Batson put unsuspecting divinity students into a moral bind.[15] They were told that the experimenter was interested in how well scholars of God could speak off the cuff. In another building (so the cover story went), a research assistant was waiting to record them making an impromptu talk. Half of the duped participants were told that they should discuss the value of seminary experience for occupations other than the ministry. The others were asked to offer some thoughts on the parable of the Good Samaritan (you know, that exemplary fellow who helped a stranger in need at the roadside). The researchers then manipulated the urgency of the students' mission by telling them either that they had a few extra minutes, that they were right on time, or that they were already late. As the innocent student set off for the other building, what did they encounter in the alleyway but a person slumped wretchedly over a wall. (Sound familiar?) With that flawless feeling for theatrics so necessary for success in social psychology, the researchers arranged for the distressed man to cough (twice) and groan as the student passed him.

What the researchers were actually interested in was which divinity students would stop to help the ailing man. Assessing the flavour and motives underlying the students' religiosity using various questionnaires, they looked to see whether this had any impact on whether students practised what the Bible preached. It did not. Indeed, their findings are hard to credit. The only factor that influenced whether the student helped was whether they thought that they had time to spare: people who thought that they had a few extra minutes to kill did generally offer assistance, but people told that they were running late almost all hurried by. Ironically, even those theologians busily making mental notes on the lessons to be learned on the road from Jerusalem to Jericho were no more likely to show compassion to the stranger. Indeed, as the researchers wryly noted, several students on their way to talk about the Good Samaritan literally stepped over the victim as they hurried on their way.

The dreadful insight into our moral frailty that this research offers us should be edifying. And yet – what do you know – our immoral brains have a way of convincing us that the regrettable moral deficiencies of others have few lessons to teach us with regard to our own saintly dispositions. Researchers described Milgram's electric-shock experiment to psychology students and then asked them to look into their souls and speculate on what they would have done in the same situation.[16] Some of the students were already rather knowledgeable about Milgram's legendary research. If they were to learn anything from his work, it was that it's not so much the kind of person you are as the pressures of the situation in which you find yourself that will determine how you behave. Yet their education failed to bring them self-enlightenment. They confidently predicted that they would defy the experimenter far earlier than would a typical volunteer.[17] Indeed, although they were also all well versed in the self-conceits to which we are susceptible, their self-portraiture, as they imagined themselves as one of Milgram's teachers, was no less flattering than that of students unschooled in both Milgram's findings and the brain's narcissism.

The problem is that you may know, intellectually, that people's moral stamina is but a leaf blown hither and thither by the winds of circumstance. You may be (and indeed now are) comprehensively informed about the self-enhancing distortions of the human brain. Yet this knowledge is almost impossible to apply to oneself. Somehow, it fails dismally to penetrate the self-image. Can you imagine yourself delivering extreme and intensely painful electric shocks to a protesting fellow human being? Of course not. I doubt if anyone reading this book can picture themselves behaving in this way. But the fact is, if you had been one of Milgram's many unsuspecting teachers, you almost certainly would have behaved just like everyone else. (Go on, admit it. Even now, you're thinking that you'd have been one of the rare people who defied the experimenter.)

Unfortunately, our refusal to acknowledge the truth in the homily 'There but for the grace of God go I' does more damage than simply keeping us peacefully smug about our own moral superiority. When we ignore the power of circumstances to overwhelm personality, we wind up misguidedly looking at a person's character in order to explain their failure to uphold an ideally high standard of conduct (the one that we ourselves would doubtless maintain).[18] And we persist in this habit, known as the correspondence bias, even when we should know better. Students shown the film of Milgram's experiments, *Obedience*, made this very mistake.[19] Instead of acknowledging the unexpected power of the experimenter's authority, they fell back on their old bad habit of presuming that a person's behaviour offers unconditional insight into his inner nature. The students watching the film inferred that there were dark, sadistic shadows lurking in the souls of Milgram's participants. This became clear in the second part of the experiment, when they were told about a variation of Milgram's research in which teachers were free to set the shock generator at whatever level they wanted. Asked to guess what level of shock teachers would use in this version of the experiment, they hugely overestimated the intensity of shocks that Milgram's participants actually delivered. By pointing the finger of blame at the person, rather than the situation, they unfairly pegged the participants as 'wolves rather than sheep', as the researchers put it.

Nor can we console ourselves by supposing that, in settings more familiar to us than a macabre psychology experiment, we do a better job of sizing up the balance of scruples and situations. Students lectured at length about the findings of the Good Samaritan experiment remained insistent that someone who scuttled past the groaning man must be particularly black of heart, rather than merely a pawn of his pressing affairs. Asked to predict how he would behave if he had time to spare, the students anticipated – wrongly – that even then he would callously disregard the victim.[20] They were no more sensitive to how we are all influenced by our current situation than were other students who knew little about the original experiment.

Our thoughtless dismissal of how the unobtrusive pressures of the scene around us can mould behaviour may cause us to depreciate others in yet another way. It puts us at risk of overlooking the impressive strength of character displayed by those rare people who do indeed manage to break free of the constraints set by their particular situations and circumstances. Thinking that any decent person (ourselves included) would have done the same, we may be heedless of the moral fibre shown by the few people who defied the commands of Milgram's experimenter to continue shocking the learner, or who, hard-pushed for time, nonetheless stopped to help someone in need.[21]

The masterful hypocrisy of the immoral brain demands a certain grudging respect. It lazily applies nothing but the most superficial and disapproving analysis of others' misdemeanours, while bending over backwards to reassure that *you* can do no wrong. Of course there is always potential for embarrassment whenever we deviate (as we inevitably do) from the impeccable ethical standards we believe ourselves to live by. As we have already seen, the brain can sometimes deal with this awkwardness by adeptly supplying excuses to explain away the unrepresentative flaws in your conduct.

But what if there are no obvious mitigating circumstances to call upon? With a little mental shuffling, there are other ways to rebalance the ledger. When we find ourselves behaving in a manner that is inconsistent with our moral code, rather than acknowledging our duplicity we can craftily adapt our beliefs to make the behaviour itself seem satisfactory after all. In the classic demonstration of these underhand accounting practices at work, volunteers spent a tedious hour emptying and refilling trays of spools, and twisting pegs quarter-turns on a board.[22] Over and over again. When the hour was finally up, the experimenter made it seem as though the study was over (although, in fact, it had hardly begun). Pushing back his chair and lighting up a cigarette, he explained that there were actually two separate groups taking part in this experiment. One half were being told beforehand, by his accomplice, that the tasks they were about to perform were interesting, intriguing and exciting. The other group (to which the participant supposedly belonged) received no such introduction. (According to the cover story, the researchers were interested in how the effusive claims made beforehand affected performance.) Feigning some embarrassment, the experimenter then asked if the participant, who'd just staggered to the end of his hour of mind-cracking tedium, would mind taking the place of the accomplice, who had failed to show up on time. All he had to do, said the experimenter, was to tell the next participant how much fun he'd just been having with the spools and the pegs. Some of the participants were offered one dollar, others twenty dollars, to tell these lies.

Almost all agreed to collude in the experimental deception. For those offered twenty dollars (a hefty sum in the 1950s when this study was done), it made perfect sense to tell an inconsequential lie for such a generous reward. Who wouldn't choose to do the same, or forgive it in another? But the participants who'd been offered only one dollar couldn't explain their behaviour in the same way. Failing to realise the subtle pressure on them to comply with the experimenter's request, they were placed in a rather uncomfortable position. On the one hand, they had just spent a dreary hour of their precious life performing stupefyingly boring tasks; on the other hand they had, for no apparent good reason, just told the next participant to hold onto her hat as the thrills began. Were they really the sort of person who would lie for a dollar? Of course not. And yet, uncomfortably inconsistent with this conviction in their good and honest character, was their awareness of the fib they had just told. In order to deal with this cognitive dissonance, as it is known, the men surreptitiously adjusted how they felt about the experiment. Asked after this part of the experiment to say, in all honesty, how interesting and enjoyable they had found it, those clutching their one paltry dollar claimed to have had a much better time than those with a roll of twenty bulging in their back pocket.

There is one final strategy available to the immoral brain as it goes about its important business of nipping in the bud, swiftly and efficiently, any moral misgivings we might otherwise experience. We can persuade ourselves that, really, there is no ethical dimension at all to the situation in which we find ourselves. This way, if there's no moral duty to be done, why should we feel bad about doing nothing? How was it that none of the 38 witnesses to a fatal stabbing of a young woman in Queens, New York, intervened or called the police? Because 'we thought it was a lovers' quarrel', said one woman. 'I went back to bed.'[23] And in covert laboratory set-ups designed to give unsuspecting participants the opportunity to showcase their social conscience, the excuses given by the many who remain apathetically idle are even more remarkable.[24] People who fail to report smoke billowing into a room suggest that it is simply smog or steam. People who don't help a woman who has just fallen off a ladder claim that she hadn't actually fallen, or wasn't really injured. Did the hurried participants in the Good Samaritan study convince themselves that the coughing, groaning wretch in the alleyway didn't really need help? Quite possibly. It's just more comfortable that way.

As any parent knows, it is a long haul from the joyful lawlessness of toddlerhood to the moral maturity of adulthood. Currently, one of my son's favourite misdeeds is to roll his baby brother from his tummy onto his back. Normally a sweet and affectionate older brother, occasionally, when parental eyes are diverted, he gives in to temptation and trundles the baby over on the play-mat. What he does next starkly exposes his childish lack of under-standing of grown-up notions of right and wrong. He does not pretend that the baby deserved it, nor blame the baby for being so seductively rotund. He does not excuse himself by calling attention to his tender age. He makes no claim that other, less pliant toddlers would flip the baby over much more frequently. Nor does he even appear to consider suggesting that the baby's tears stem from joy, rather than shocked bewilderment at finding himself unexpectedly staring at the ceiling. Instead, he does something that no self-respecting adult brain would ever permit.

He chastens himself with a cry of 'Naughty Isaac!' and, with genuine humility, places himself in the naughty corner.

He has much to learn.

CHAPTER 4

The Deluded Brain

A slapdash approach to the truth

When learned psychiatrists gathered together to brainstorm their way to an official description of delusions, they had a terrible time trying to come up with a definition that didn't make a large proportion of the population instantly eligible for psychiatric services.[1] One can imagine the increasingly frustrated attempts to position the line appropriately between sanity and madness. Dr Smith might kick off with her own pet definition of delusion.

'I'm going to suggest *a false belief.*'

We can envisage Dr Brown instantly reeking of sarcasm.

'Wonderful! Now I shall be able to cure all of my paranoid patients instantly, simply by arranging for them to be properly persecuted.'

Cunningly, Dr Smith adjusts her original definition to suit.

'*And*, as I was just about to add, this must be *a false belief held despite evidence to the contrary.*'

Dr Brown's scorn continues unabated.

'Oh, I see. Such as, for example, your tenaciously held views on the beneficial effects of psychoanalysis for manic-depression!'

Dr Smith hits back in the most ferocious fashion available to academics.

'Well, if it's that recent article of yours in the *Journal of Psychiatry* you think should have changed my mind, I hardly consider that a convincing source of contrary evidence!'

At this point one imagines a third party, let us call her Dr Jones, stepping in smoothly.

'Doctors, please! What about *a false belief held despite incontrovertible and obvious evidence to the contrary*?'

And so on and so forth until the coffee break.

The trouble is, the question of evidence doesn't help much. No one can prove to a psychotic patient that the devil *isn't* in fact transmitting thoughts into his head, any more than they can prove wrong the 150 million Americans who think it possible for someone to be physically possessed by the devil. (Or, before entire nations start scoffing, the 25 million Britons who believe in communication with the dead.) But we can't allow everyone with a common or garden belief in the paranormal to be defined into madness – there simply aren't enough psychiatrists to cope. And perhaps that's why the definition of delusion has, tacked onto it, the proviso that it must be a belief that almost no one else holds. So let us, like the little green men who swoop down in flying saucers to take a closer look at us, probe a little deeper …

Our beliefs range from the run-of-the-mill to the strikingly bizarre, and many at each end of the spectrum embrace their own share of deviance from reality. Our first problem is that we are, at root, very poor scientists. All sorts of biases slip in unnoticed as we form and test our beliefs, and these tendencies lead us astray to a surprising degree. Of course, an ignoble agenda – the desire to see evidence for a belief we'd secretly prefer to hold –

can wreak its prejudicing influence on our opinions. However, even when we genuinely seek the truth, our careless data collection and appraisal can leave us in woeful error about ourselves, other people and the world. Then consider our susceptibility to strange experiences. After all, hallucinations, déjà vu, premonitions, depersonalisation and religious experiences are not uncommon in the general population.[2] Add these to our innate lack of scientific rigour and you have a perilous combination. And, it's not yet clear exactly what it is that saves most of us from crossing the shadowy line that separates everyday delusions from the clinical variety.

Evidence that our brains are deluded begins with a seemingly innocuous question: Are you happy with your social life? Or, to put it another way, are you unhappy with your social life?

Your answer, you may be surprised to learn, is astonishingly sensitive to which way the question is phrased. People asked if they are happy, rather than unhappy, with their social lives report greater satisfaction.[3] Responsibility for this peculiar irrationality in our self-knowledge lies with what is known as the positive test strategy. As we contemplate that fascinating inner tangle of our attitudes, personality traits and skills, we ask our internal oracle questions to divine what we suppose to be the truth about ourselves. Am I happy with my social life? Do I want to stay married? Would I make a good parent? You then trawl through your store of self-knowledge searching for evidence that the hypothesis in question is correct. You remember that party you enjoyed last weekend. The touching interest your spouse takes in the small potatoes of your life. Your remarkable talent for manipulating balloons into the shape of animals.

Phrase the question the other way round, however, and your memory throws up a very different pile of evidence. Am I *un*happy with my social life? Now you remember what bores you find most of your friends. Do I want a divorce? You think of that dreadful silent meal on your anniversary. Would I make a bad parent? Suddenly your unfortunate tendency to leave precious possessions behind on public transport springs to mind. And that's why people asked if they're happy – rather than unhappy – with their social lives believe themselves to be more blessed on that front. (The positive test strategy is also the reason you should never ask someone you want to stay with, 'Don't you love me anymore?')

We use the positive test strategy to test hypotheses about others as well as ourselves, with similarly distorting effects. Crucial decisions may fall one way or another as a consequence of something as trivial as which way round the question is phrased. People's views about child custody cases, for example, can yield very different outcomes depending on whether they are asked 'Which parent should have custody of the child?', or 'Which parent should be *denied* custody of the child?'[4] In this classic experiment, Parent A was moderately well equipped for custody in all respects: income, health, working hours, rapport with the child and social life. Parent B, in contrast, had a rather more sporadic parental profile. On the one hand, Parent B had an above average income and a very close relationship with the child. But on the other hand, this parent had an extremely active social life, a great deal of work-related travel and minor health problems. When people were asked who should have custody of the child, they followed the positive test strategy of searching for evidence that each parent would be a good custodian. As a result, Parent B's impressive credentials with regard to income and relationship with the child shone out over Parent A's more modest abilities on these fronts, and nearly two-thirds of participants plumped for Parent B as the best custodian.

Ask who should be *denied* custody, however, and a very different picture emerges. The positive test strategy yielded evidence of Parent B's inadequacies as a guardian: the busy social and work life, and the health problems. By comparison, a positive test strategy search of Parent A's more pedestrian profile offered no strong reasons for rejection as a guardian. The result: the majority of participants decided to deny Parent B custody.

You may be relieved to be assured that the positive test strategy has an effect only if there is genuine uncertainty in your mind about the issue you're considering. It's not going to make much difference whether you ask a feminist if they approve of unequal pay for men and women, or whether they disapprove. Nonetheless, the implication of the positive test strategy research is rather worrisome, suggesting as it does that many difficult choices in our lives, based on our inferences about ourselves and others, might perhaps have swung the other way if we had only considered them from the opposite angle.

A second damaged tool in all of our personal scientific toolboxes is the brain software we use to spot correlations. Correlation is what put the warning messages onto packets of cigarettes.

There are plenty of 80-year-olds puffing away on a couple of packs a day but, on the whole, the more you smoke the more likely it is that the Grim Reaper will scythe in your direction sooner rather than later. If *everyone* who smoked died instantly from lung cancer then the tobacco companies might not have been able to kid on for so long that smoking was a harmless hobby. But because nature is messy and complicated, correlations are very difficult to spot by eye. It took statistical analysis to pinpoint the relationship between smoking and cancer.

You may not want to blame your brain for not coming equipped with the full functionality of a statistical analysis program. However, you may want to get a little shirty about your brain's little habit of making up statistical results. Your brain has a sneaky tendency to 'see' the correlations that it expects to see, but which aren't actually there. This is called illusory correlation and the classic demonstration of it in action was provided way back in 1969, using the Rorschach inkblot test.[5] At that time, Rorschach's inkblots were very much in vogue as a diagnostic tool for psychoanalysts. The idea behind this hoary and infamous test is that what you see in the carefully designed splodges of ink reveals some well-hidden horror of your psyche to the psychoanalyst. While you are innocently spotting butterflies and faces, thinking it a pleasant ice-breaker before the real work begins, the psychoanalyst is listening to the sweet ker-CHING! of the therapy till.

Back in the sixties when this experiment took place, homosexuality was still regarded as a mental illness, and therapists had all sorts of ideas about what homosexuals tended to see in the inkblots. The experimenters surveyed 32 experienced clinicians, asking them what they had noticed in their homosexual clients when they used the inkblots. Almost half of the clinicians said that these patients tended to see 'anal content', to use the unhappily evocative phrase employed in the field. However, scientific research even at that time showed that there was no such relationship: homosexual men are no more likely to see butts in blots than are heterosexuals. To try to understand why the clinicians were making this mistake, the researchers gave first-year psychology students some fake clinical experience. The students read through 30 fictitious case-notes, like the example overleaf. Each case-note showed first an inkblot, then what the patient claimed to have seen in the inkblot (in this example, 'horse's rear end'), and the patient's two chief emotional symptoms. (Remember, we're back in the era when homosexuality was regarded as a mental illness.)

The case-notes were cleverly designed to ensure that, over all the case-notes, there was no correlation whatsoever between having homosexual feelings and seeing something to do with bottoms in the blots. Yet when the researchers asked the students whether they'd noticed any relationship between homosexual tendencies and seeing certain sorts of things in the blots, over half of the students reported seeing a correlation with rear-ends. The students saw the very same illusory correlation as did the experienced clinicians. They saw what wasn't there. In fact, this mistaken belief persisted even when, on another occasion, the case-notes were arranged such that homosexuals were *less* likely to report anal content than were heterosexual clients.

PATIENT X

'horse's rear end'

The man who said this:

Has strong feelings of inferiority.

Feels sexual feelings towards other men.

Note: For reasons of copyright, the above inkblot is not a genuine Rorschach inkblot and has been created for this book for illustration purposes only.

This experiment should have had the clinicians blushing into their beards. (It was the dawn of the seventies and they were psychoanalysts: of course they had beards.) Despite their many years of professional experience, the clinicians turned out to be working with the same facile and erroneous hypothesis that first-year psychology students developed during a 30-minute experiment. The reason was illusory correlation. On the surface it seemed like a plausible hypothesis. Gay men talking about bottoms: who needs Dr Freud to work that one out? With a deceptively convincing hypothesis embedded in your skull, it is but one short step for your brain to start seeing evidence for that hypothesis. Your deluded brain sees what it expects to see, not what is actually there. The moral? Treat with the greatest suspicion the proof of your own eyes.

Our memories also warrant a guarded scepticism since they, too, can weakly succumb to our mistaken expectations. We might, for example, eagerly look forward to impressive improvements in our concentration, note-taking, reading, study and work-scheduling skills after investing our time in one of those 'study skills' courses so frequently offered by universities. Students about to be treated to a three-week study skills programme were asked to rate their studying abilities before the course started.[6] Similarly able students who were put on a waiting list for this popular self-improvement programme were asked to do exactly the same. Then, after the first group had completed the course, both groups were asked to say whether they felt that their scholarly talents had improved over the period of the programme. (The only skill the waiting-list students had got to practise during this time was, of course, waiting.) Everyone was also asked to remember, as accurately as they could, how they had rated those very same skills three weeks before. Their heads buzzing with handy tips on skimming, power-listening and mind-maps, the students fresh from the programme were confident that they were now a superior breed of scholar. Yet curiously, they did no better in the exams and term grades that followed than did the students uninitiated in the secrets of successful swotting. So how, then, were they able to convince themselves of real increase in skills? Despite the course being ineffective, the students managed to persuade themselves by exaggerating how poor their study skills were before the programme. Asked to recall how they had evaluated their learning abilities before the programme, they remembered giving themselves worse ratings than they actually had. In other words, by memory's sleight of hand they gave themselves a little extra room for improvement.

Nor did the collusion of memory with blithe optimistic hope end there. Six months later, a researcher rang to ask them about their academic performance following the course. So willing were the students' memories to fall in with their great expectations for the study skills course that unlike the waiting-list students they remembered doing better than they actually had. Working on the assumption that the techniques they had zealously mastered on the course must have helped their grades, the students manufactured evidence to prove it. The researchers speculate that this sort of helpful rewriting of personal history to fit in with people's expectations of self-improvement might help to explain the enduring popularity of self-help programmes of dubious objective value.

A further problem with our beliefs is the irrational loyalty that we show towards them. Once acquired, even the most erroneous beliefs enjoy an undeserved degree of protection from rejection and revision (as revealed in the next chapter).

So, what with our proclivity towards seeking evidence that supports whichever hypothesis we happen to be entertaining, our penchant for simply inventing supporting evidence, and our pig-headed retention of beliefs, it's easy to see how our unsound scientific strategies can have unhappy consequences. It all bodes very ill for the accuracy of the beliefs to which we are led.[7] Yet these distortions pale into insignificance when stood beside clinical delusions. Thinking yourself a little less happy with your social life than you actually are is not in the same ballpark as believing yourself dead (the Cotard delusion described in 'The Emotional Brain'). Falling prey to an illusory correlation between your moods and your menstrual cycle[8] simply does not compare with the delusional belief that your thoughts are being controlled by the devil. And misjudging your spouse's fitness to continue in the role as your life companion does not hold a candle to the belief, known as the Capgras delusion, that your spouse (or other family member) has been replaced by an alien, robot or clone.

The false beliefs of the delusional patient are simply of a different order of magnitude to our own modest misconceptions. Yet it has proved remarkably difficult to establish what the difference is between, say, the Capgras patient who is convinced that her husband has been replaced by a robot, and the person who goes no further than occasionally fantasising about the joys of a Stepford spouse. Until quite recently, the psychoanalytic crew were having a field day with the Capgras delusion. According to their way of looking at the delusion, it is the subconsciously held feelings of ambivalence towards a family member that are help-fully resolved by the belief that the person has been replaced by an impostor. Voila! A bona fide reason to no longer love your mother. However, recent progress in cognitive neuropsychiatry has put a few spanners in the psychodynamic works.[9] For one thing, Capgras patients often show signs of brain injury, which suggests that it isn't simply their subconscious playing up. More-over, some Capgras patients also claim that personal belongings have been replaced – and it's hard to describe convincingly the subconscious hatred a patient has towards his watch or, as in one curious case, a tube of Polyfilla.[10]

Then an exciting discovery was made: Capgras patients aren't emotionally aroused by familiar people.[11] Normally, when you see someone you know, your skin conductance response increases, showing that that person is of some emotional signifi-cance to you. But Capgras patients don't produce this emotional buzz. Could this be the key to their delusion? Some psychologists have suggested that it is. The Capgras patient recognises the per-son in front of them ('Well, it certainly *looks* like my husband …') but, because of brain injury, gets no emotional tingle from the experience ('… but it doesn't *feel* like my husband'). In order to explain this strange emotional lack, the patient concludes that the person in front of them must be an impostor of some sort.[12] In other words, at least part of the reason that you have never woken up one morning, looked at your husband, and then twitched open the nets in search of the spaceship he came in on is that your brain is intact. You may not be thrown into a fit of passion by his crazy bedhead hairstyle, but you will at least produce the minimally required level of sweat when you see his face.

But can this really be the whole story? The Capgras belief is so irrational, so impossible, so – let's just say it – nutty, that it's hard to understand why the patients themselves don't immediately reject as ludicrous nonsense the idea that their husband or wife has been replaced by an alien. Especially since the patients themselves can be intelligently coherent, and well aware of how far their assertion strains credulity.[13] Nonetheless they politely maintain that, in their case, it just so happens to be true. What is it, then, that pushes delusional patients over the brink?

One idea is that part of the problem for delusional patients is that they are even worse everyday scientists than we are. One hypothesis along these lines is that delusional patients jump to conclusions.[14] Instead of sampling a decent amount of data before forming a belief, the delusional patient leaps foolhardily to their half-baked conclusion on the flimsiest of evidence. Intuitively, this makes sense. After all, how much evidence can the Capgras patient actually have for his claim that his wife has been replaced by a robot? The classic test used to put to the proof the jumping-to-conclusions hypothesis is known as the Beads Task.[15] Follow the instructions on the next page and take a turn yourself – if you dare.

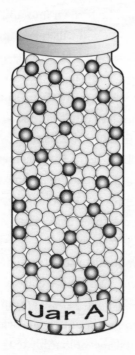 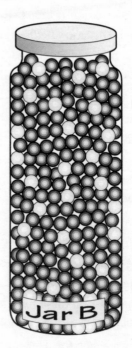

Here are two jars of beads – A and B. Jar A has 85 white beads and 15 black beads. Jar B has 85 black beads and 15 white beads. Beads will be drawn from the same jar each time. Your task is to decide which jar the beads are being drawn from. You can see as many beads as you like to be completely sure which jar has been chosen.

On the following page is a list of beads drawn from the mystery jar. Place your hand over it. Then, when you're ready, slide your hand down until you can see the first bead. Keep on slowly moving down until you have seen enough beads to be confident which jar they came from. Then count the number of beads you saw and turn to the next page.

black bead

black bead

black bead

white bead

black bead

black bead

black bead

black bead

black bead

white bead

white bead

In these studies people generally ask for between three and four beads before they feel confident enough to say that the beads are being drawn from Jar B (you did choose Jar B, I hope?). It's probably close to the number of beads that you yourself chose. However, in the eyes of a statistician you would have been going on looking at bead after bead for a pathetically timid length of time. The probability of the bead being from Jar B after the first black bead is a whopping 85 per cent. After the second black bead, this increases to 97 per cent. At this point, the statistician claims to have seen enough, and impatiently waves the jars away. You and I, however, carry on to the next bead, and the next, just to get that additional tiny extra likelihood of being correct. In contrast, people suffering from delusions only request about two beads before making their decision. In other words, they are better 'scientists' than we are.[16] Back to the drawing board.

But wait! In a study of all that can go wrong with reasoning, Professors Wason and Johnson-Laird describe the 'repetition, asseveration, self-contradiction, outright denial of the fact, and ritualistic behaviour' that they observed in a group of people whose reasoning was so poor that they fetched up as material for a book chapter bluntly entitled 'Pathology of Reasoning'.[17] This sounds promising. Here's one of the tasks. Participants were told that the sequence of three numbers (called a triad) '2 4 6' fulfilled a simple relational rule chosen by the experimenter. The participants' task was to try to work out what the rule was by offering their own patterns of three numbers. After each triad they were told whether or not it conformed to the rule. People were told to announce their hypothesis about what the rule was only when they were confident that they were correct. The rule was that the numbers had to get bigger as they went along (or, as the professors preferred to put it, 'numbers increase in order of magnitude'). It could hardly have been simpler. (As Professor Johnson-Laird may well have remarked to his colleague, 'Elementary, my dear Wason.') Yet take a look at the tortured performance of the person who proffered three increasingly convoluted hypotheses before giving up in defeat nearly an hour later (a few examples of triads offered are given before the hypotheses):

8 13 15 [correct]
1 2031 2033 [correct]
'The rule is that the first and second numbers are random, and the third is the second plus two.'

4 5 7 [correct]
9 5 7 [incorrect]
263 364 366 [correct]
'The rule is that the first and second numbers are random, but the first is smaller than the second, and the third is the second plus two.'

41 43 42 [incorrect]
41 43 67 [correct]
67 43 45 [incorrect]
'The rule is that the second number is random, and either the first number equals the second minus two, and the third is random but greater than the second; or the third number equals the second plus two, and the first is random but less than the second.'

What did Professors Wason and Johnson-Laird make of this con-voluted performance? 'It is not difficult to detect strong obsessional features ...', they remark. 'He offers merely three formulations ... within a space of 50 minutes, and finally arrives at a complex disjunction which largely preserves the remnants of previous hypotheses. These are strong hints that his fertile imagination, and intense preoccupation with original hypotheses, has narrowed his field of appreciation to the point where he has become blind to the obvious.'

Well! Blind to the obvious, eh? Doesn't that just describe delu-sional patients to a T. They get it stuck into their heads that their wife is a cloned replacement, and nothing will persuade them otherwise. Have Wason and Johnson-Laird found the holy grail of a reasoning abnormality in patients with delusions? It certainly looks like it, but for one small problem. Not one of their partici-pants was mentally ill. They were university students in tip-top psychological condition. In the particular example I described, the volunteer was a male undergraduate from Stanford University.

In fact, on the whole, delusional patients tend to do just as well (or rather, just as badly) as we do on reasoning tests.[18] This has resulted in a rather cantankerous academic debate. Everyone agrees that delusional patients often have a very strange experience of which they must try to make sense: the Capgras patient has to explain why his wife no longer feels familiar; the Cotard patient has to account for her overwhelming detachment from her sense of self. But on one side of the debate there are the researchers who think it obvious that there must also be something odd about the reasoning abilities of somebody who can believe, for example, that they don't exist. How else could they entertain such a fantastical belief?[19] Others, though, in response, merely wave an expansive hand towards the bulky testimony to the sorry irrationality of the healthy brain and ask, what more is needed?[20]

The idea that we are no more rational than the pathologically deluded may not appeal greatly to our vanity, yet it remains an intriguing possibility. 'The seeds of madness can be planted in anyone's backyard', is the claim of psychologist Philip Zimbardo who, metaphorical trowel in hand, has dug hard for evidence to prove it.[21] The backyards he chose were those of 50 happy, healthy and highly hypnotisable Stanford students. The seed of madness sown was the peculiar sensation of feeling strangely and unaccountably aroused. Zimbardo did this by hypnotising his volunteers. Once they were in a hypnotic state, the students were told that when they heard a buzzer go off they would act as if they were aroused. Their hearts would begin to race, and they would breathe more heavily. Some of the students were told that they would of course remember that they were feeling this way because of the hypnotic suggestion that they had just received. But other students, in the 'amnesic' condition, were told by the mesmerising experimenter that they would have no memory for why they were feeling agitated, but that they should try to think of possible explanations for their bodily tizz. They were then given a gentle hint as to where the cause might lie; they were offered one of the sorts of explanations we frequently use to make sense of our sensations and emotions. Some were told that it might have something to do with the physical environment. Others were asked to consider their bodies as a possible source of their internal perturbation. To yet another group of students, the experimenter intimated that the explanation might lie with other people.

As we saw in 'The Emotional Brain', we have no particularly privileged information as to why we are feeling emotionally stirred. Our agitation does not come pre-labelled – we have to match it up with a likely trigger. And if the true cause of your jittery feeling is unknown to you (the waiter forgot that you ordered a decaf), or is one that you would prefer to ignore (no longer in the first bloom of youth, even the gentle slope up your street puts you in a puff), you will plump for any other plausible-sounding explanation. Potentially, this way madness lies, according to Zimbardo. The hypnotised students became aroused right on cue with the sound of the buzzer. Next, they worked their way through several well-known psychological tests, designed to roughly locate the volunteer's mental state on the line between sanity and madness. Finally, and still under hypnotic suggestion, the volunteers talked with the experimenter for a quarter of an hour about how they were feeling, and why they might be feeling that way. This interview was videotaped, and afterwards ten clinical psychologists (who knew nothing about the experiment) watched the tapes and scrutinised the students' behaviour and conversation for telltale signs of derangement.

Unsurprisingly, the volunteers allowed to remember why they were feeling aroused dealt with the experiment with sane equanimity. The amnesic volunteers, however, who had no obvious hook on which to hang their feelings, struggled to cope with the situation. The Stanford students whose hypnotic suggestion included the pointer that their environment might hold the key, scanned and searched their surroundings like terrified lab-rats. 'I really think that the fumes of the projector kind of made me sick ... the ink fumes ... not the ink fumes ... maybe it was just the warm air', was a typical sort of speculation for people in this group. The unexplained arousal, together with the pointer to the environment, made them feel that the surroundings were charged with danger: their scores on a scale of phobic thoughts were the same as those of patients suffering from full-blown clinical phobias. Students encouraged to look to their bodies for an explanation actually outscored clinical hypochondriacs (whose corporeal preoccupations earn them a psychiatric diagnosis) on a questionnaire measure of bodily concerns. 'My muscles are a bit tense and I have a headache ... I think it is because of today's early swimming practice ... or maybe from horseback riding', were the thoughts of one student catapulted into bodily fixation by the experimental manipulation.

But it was the suggestion to focus on people that seemed to spark the most extreme responses. These students became paranoid, hostile and vindictive, according to the clinical psychologists watching the taped interviews. Despite being alone in the laboratory when they became aroused, the students attributed their excitation to recent confrontations, to jealousy, to anger with others. Indeed, so unusual was their behaviour that the professional clinicians confidently diagnosed fully 80 per cent of these students as pathologically disturbed, labelling them officially insane. Disoriented and distraught, the volunteers in this experiment (and others similar to it) 'became inarticulate, confused, hyperactive, angrily banging on the desk, in near tears, fright-

ened, picking away at a scab, anxious, or developing an uncontrollable muscle tic'. Yet seconds later, when their memory of the
hypnotic suggestion was restored, their 'madness' lifted. Briefly
confused, the debriefed volunteers smiled and laughed in aston-
ishment at the strangeness of the ideas they had just had. No
harm done. But of course when there is no cunning researcher
available to magic away with a flourish the source of your dis-
orientation, the seedlings of insanity can take root and flourish.

This is not an experiment that reassures us, exposing as it does
the disturbing ease and speed with which brains (even smart, edu-
cated Stanford brains) can fall in with theories that have no basis
in fact. (We may also raise an eyebrow or two at the alacrity with
which the clinical psychologists diagnosed clinical syndromes in
a substantial proportion of these momentarily bewildered young
people.) Disquieting too is the powerful mental disruption
stirred up by something that seems likely enough to befall any of
us at some point in our lives – an inexplicable feeling of heightened arousal. If this should happen, what – we must worry –
would save our own sane selves from developing the irrational
dread of the phobic patient, the pathological fixation on an illusory medical condition, or the frenzied suspicions of the para-
noiac?[22] Suddenly these pathological beliefs seem only a small
step away from the wide berth so many of us take care to give
harmless spiders, unfounded worries about mystifying aches and
twinges, or the intriguing theories we entertain regarding the
motives of our friends, family and colleagues.

But we mustn't relinquish our sense of rational superiority
too quickly. After all, psychiatrists recognise that some delusions

(the non-bizarre variety) are beliefs about real-life situations that could be true (some people do become terminally ill, for instance, and some people are conspired against), but just happen to be groundless, or greatly exaggerated. But what of the bizarre delusions that have no footing at all in reality? Your wife has been replaced by a robot. You are dead. Aliens are controlling your thoughts. True, some of the wiring within the brain may have gone wrong, leaving such patients with experiences that are very much out of the ordinary. But surely that cannot be the only problem? Take, for example, the delusion of control often suffered by patients with schizophrenia. They believe that their thoughts, actions and impulses are being controlled by an external force, such as an alien, or radar. Some researchers think that the problem lies in the patient's inability to keep tabs on his intentions: to brush his hair, stir his tea, pick up a pen.[23] This means that he is no longer able to tell the difference between actions he has willed, and actions that are done to him. Because he can no longer match an action with his intention to perform it, it feels as if it is externally caused. Struggling to explain this strange experience, the patient decides that some external agent is now in command of him. Aliens are puppeteering his mind.

This does not seem like the sort of hypothesis that someone with all their reasoning faculties intact would entertain for a moment. The idea that an alien is controlling your brain goes straight into the box marked 'Mad People Only'. Right? But consider what I will call the 'alien hand' experiment.[24] The volunteers (normal, mentally healthy Danes) did a task in which they had to track a target with a joystick, and they could see on a screen how they were doing. But on certain trials, unbeknown to them and by means of ingenious guile, the volunteers saw a false hand instead of their own. The hand moved in time with the volunteer's actual hand, but it was deliberately designed to miss the target. It didn't do quite what the volunteers were telling their own hand to do. After the experiment, the volunteers were asked to explain their poor performance on the false hand trials. Here are some examples of the explanations suggested by the sane Danes:

'It was done by magic.'

'My hand took over and my mind was not able to control it.'

'I was hypnotised.'

'I tried hard to make my hand go to the left, but my hand tried harder and was able to overcome me and went off to the right.'

'My hand was controlled by an outside physical force – I don't know what it was, but I could feel it.'

Remember, these were normal, psychiatrically healthy people experiencing a slight and brief discrepancy between their motor commands and their perceptual experience. This is nothing in comparison with the continually discombobulating experiences of the patient with schizophrenia. Yet it was enough for at least some of the mentally healthy Danish participants to invoke the powers of hypnosis, magic and external forces, in order to explain the modest waywardness of a single appendage.

The fanciful explanations conjured up by the volunteers in the alien hand experiment may seem surprising. Yet around half of the general, psychiatrically healthy population have faith in the powers of paranormal phenomena, such as witchcraft, voodoo, the occult or telepathy.[25] And why not alien forces? Half of the American public claims to believe that aliens have abducted humans. Presumably these 150 million people would have no reason to think that body-snatching extraterrestrials would draw the line at interfering with a Danish psychology experiment.[26]

The frequency of odd experiences in our everyday lives may go some way towards explaining the popularity of peculiar beliefs. As it turns out, strange experiences of the type suffered by clinically deluded patients are quite common in the general population. In one recent survey, mentally healthy participants were asked about odd experiences they might have had, and the 40 experiences that they were offered to pick from were based on actual clinical delusions.[27] For example, they were asked, 'Do your thoughts ever feel alien to you in some way?' and 'Have your thoughts ever been so vivid that you were worried other people would hear them?'. The average participant admitted to having had over 60 per cent of these 'delusional' experiences. What's more, one in ten participants reported *more* such experiences than did a group of psychotic patients who were actually suffering from pathological delusions. Combine these common strange experiences in the general population with the unfortunate irrationality of the healthy brain – its biased and unscientific approach to evaluating hypotheses – and you begin to understand the blurring of the line between pathological delusions and the normal deluded brain.

At no point, perhaps, does that line become more blurred than when beliefs are based on religious experiences. It is a tricky task to differentiate between faith and insanity without being somewhat subjective about it.[28] Mental health professionals are not much concerned by the devout Christian who has been fortunate enough to experience the presence of Jesus. But if the identity of that presence happens to be Elvis, rather than the son of God, then eyebrows begin to be raised. And while Catholics can safely divulge to psychiatrists their belief that God lends them the strength to pursue the Catholic way of life, Mormons should think twice before revealing their conviction that they will be transformed into a god after they die. It is fine to be assisted by a supernatural entity, but not to aspire to *be* one.

Despite our irrationality, despite the oddities of our experiences, most of us nonetheless manage to remain *compos mentis*. Yet, as this chapter has shown, it is still not clear what it is that prevents the seeds of madness from germinating in our minds. Certainly it does not seem that we have a razor-sharp rationality to thank for quickly felling any tentatively sprouting seedlings of insanity. Perhaps in some cases our strange experiences are less intense, less compelling, than those suffered by people who go on to develop full-blown clinical delusions.[29] At other times, perhaps, it's our personality, our emotional state or our social situation that gives us greater strength to cope with odd experiences and that keeps us from seeking psychiatric help.[30] And sometimes, perhaps, the grace that saves us from a psychiatric diagnosis is nothing more than the sheer good fortune that millions of others happen to share our delusion.

CHAPTER 5

The Pigheaded Brain

Loyalty a step too far

On the matter of the correct receptacle for draining spaghetti, my husband demonstrates a bewildering pigheadedness. He insists that the colander is the appropriate choice, despite the manifest ease with which the strands escape through the draining holes. Clearly the sieve, with its closer-knit design, is a superior utensil for this task. Yet despite his stone blindness to the soggy tangle of spaghetti clogging the plug-hole in the sink that results from *his* method, my husband claims to be able to observe starchy molecules clinging to the weave of the sieve for weeks and weeks after I've drained pasta in it. We have had astonishingly lengthy discussions on this issue – I have provided here merely the briefest of overviews – but after four years of marriage, the problem remains unresolved. By which of course I mean that my husband hasn't yet realised that I'm right.

The longevity of these sorts of disagreements is well known to us all. I can confidently predict that until somebody invents a colander–sieve hybrid, we will not be able to serve spaghetti to guests. The writer David Sedaris, describing an argument with his partner over whether someone's artificial hand was made of rubber or plastic, also foresaw no end to their disagreement:

'I hear you guys broke up over a plastic hand', people would say, and my rage would renew itself. The argument would continue until one of us died, and even then it would manage to wage on. If I went first, my tombstone would read IT WAS RUBBER. He'd likely take the adjacent plot and buy a larger tombstone reading NO, IT WAS PLASTIC.[1]

What is it about our brains that makes them so loyal to their beliefs? We saw in 'The Vain Brain' how we keep unpalatable information about ourselves from deflating our egos. The same sorts of tricks that keep us big-headed also underlie our tendency to be pigheaded. The brain biases, evades, twists, discounts, misinterprets, even makes up evidence – all so that we can retain that satisfying sense of being in the right. It's not only our long-cherished beliefs that enjoy such devoted loyalty from our brains. Even the most hastily formed opinion receives undeserved protection from revision. It takes only a few seconds to formulate the unthinking maxim that 'a sieve should never get its bottom wet', but a lifetime isn't long enough to correct it. I think what I like most about everything you'll find in this chapter is that if you find it unconvincing, that simply serves better to prove its point.

Our pigheadedness begins at the most basic level – the information to which we expose ourselves. Who, for example, reads the *Daily Mail*? It's – well, you know – *Daily Mail* readers. People who like to begin sentences with, 'Call me politically incorrect if you will, but …'. We don't seek refreshing challenges to our political and social ideologies from the world; we much prefer people, books, newspapers and magazines that share our own enlightened values. Surrounding ourselves with yes men in this way limits the chances of our views being contradicted. Nixon supporters had to take this strategy to drastic levels during the US Senate Watergate hearings. As evidence mounted of political burglary, bribery, extortion and other hobbies unseemly for a US President, a survey showed that the Nixon supporters developed a convenient loss of interest in politics.[2] In this way, they were able to preserve their touching faith in Nixon's suitability as a leader of their country. (In contrast, Americans who had opposed Nixon's presidency couldn't lap up the hearings quick enough.)

Our blinkered surveying of the world is only the beginning, however. Inevitably we are directly confronted with challenges to our beliefs, be it the flat-earther's view of the gentle downward curve of the sea at the horizon, a weapons inspector returning empty-handed from Iraq, or a plughole clogged with spaghetti. Yet even in the face of counter-evidence, our beliefs are protected as tenderly as our egos. Like any information that pokes a sharp stick at our self-esteem, evidence that opposes our beliefs is subjected to close, critical and almost inevitably dismissive scrutiny. In 1956, a physician called Alice Stewart published a preliminary report of a vast survey of children who had died of cancer.[3] The results from her work were clear. Just one X-ray of an unborn baby doubled the risk of childhood cancer. A mere 24 years later, the major US medical associations officially recommended that zapping pregnant women with ionising radiation should no longer be a routine part of prenatal care. (Britain took a little extra time to reach this decision.)

Why did it take so long for the medical profession to accept that a dose of radiation might not be what the doctor should be ordering for pregnant women? A strong hint comes from several experiments showing that we find research convincing and sound if the results happen to confirm our point of view. However, we will find the exact same research method shoddy and flawed if the results fail to accord with our opinions. For example, people either for or against the death penalty were asked to evaluate two research studies.[4] One showed that the death penalty was an effective deterrent against crime, the other showed that it was not. One research design compared crime rates in the same US states before and after the introduction of capital punishment. The other compared crime rates across neighbouring states with and without the death penalty. Which research strategy people found the most scientifically valid depended mostly on whether or not the study supported their views on the death penalty. Evidence that fits with our beliefs is quickly waved through the mental border control. Counter-evidence, on the other hand, must submit to close interrogation and even then will probably not be allowed in.[5] As a result, people can wind up holding their beliefs even more strongly after seeing counter-evidence. It's as if we think, 'Well, if *that's* the best that the other side can come up with then I really must be right.' This phenomenon, called belief polarisation, may help to explain why attempting to disillusion people of their perverse misconceptions is so often futile.

It would be comforting to learn that scientists and doctors, in whose hands we daily place our health and lives, are unsusceptible to this kind of partisanship. I remember being briskly reprimanded by Mr Cohen, my A-level physics teacher, for describing the gradient of a line in a graph as 'dramatic'. Mr Cohen sternly informed me that there was no element of the dramatic in science. A fact was a plain fact, not some thespian prancing around on a stage. Yet a graph that contradicts the beliefs, publications and career of a scientist is anything but a 'plain fact'. Which is why scientific papers, identical in all respects but the results, are far more likely to be found to be flawed and unpublishable if the findings disagree with the reviewer's own theoretical viewpoint.[6]

Was this part of the reason that Alice Stewart's research on X-rays received such a stony reception? In her biography she recalls, 'I became notorious. One radiobiologist commented, "Stewart used to do good work, but now she's gone senile."'[7] Unfortunately for Stewart, a later study run by a different researcher failed to find a link between prenatal X-rays and childhood cancer. Even though the design of this study had substantial defects – as the researcher himself later admitted – the medical community gleefully acclaimed it as proof that they were right and Alice Stewart was wrong. The similarity of this story to the experimental demonstrations of biased evaluation of evidence is, well, dramatic.

Eventually, of course, we got to the point we are at today, where a pregnant woman is likely to start rummaging in her handbag for her mace should an obstetrician even breathe the word 'X-ray' in earshot. But it took a very long time to get there. By 1977, there was a huge amount of research showing a link between prenatal X-rays and childhood cancer. Yet the US National Council on Radiation Protection remained stubbornly convinced that X-rays were harmless. They suggested an alternative explanation. It wasn't that radiation caused cancer. Ludicrous idea! No, the relationship between X-rays and cancer was due to the supernatural prophetic diagnostic powers of obstetricians. The obstetricians were X-raying babies they somehow *knew* would get cancer. This logically possible, yet nonetheless stubbornly porcine, hypothesis merits but one response: Oink, oink.

It's not just other people's arguments to which we turn the cold shoulder. Once we have made up our minds on a matter, arguments in favour of a contrary view – even points generated by our own brains – are abandoned by the wayside. Remember the volunteers in the study described in 'The Vain Brain', who were set to work thinking about a choice in their life?[8] Some students, you may recall, were asked to reflect on a decision they had already made (to book a holiday, or end a relationship, for example). In retrospect, had they done the right thing? Other students deliberated over a dilemma they had yet to resolve. As they sat in quiet contemplation, both groups jotted down all their thoughts. Afterwards, the researchers counted up the different sorts of thoughts listed by the students, in order to build up a picture of what their minds were up to during this phase of the experiment. The people who were still uncertain as to whether to forge ahead with a particular course of action were impressively even-handed in their weighing-up of the pros and cons, the risks and benefits. But the other students, in response to the experimenter's request to them to inwardly debate the wisdom of their choice, were careful to avoid overhearing any whispered regrets of their mind. Presumably they too had once pondered both sides of the matter before making their final decision. But they were mulishly reluctant to do so now. The researchers, totting up tallies of the different sorts of thoughts the thinkers produced, found that the 'post-decision' volunteers were far less likely to set their wits to work on the potentially awkward issue of whether or not they had done the right thing. And on the rare occasions their minds did roam towards this dangerous area, they far preferred to dwell on the positive, rather than negative, repercussions of what they had done. So what *were* their minds up to? Procrastinating, it seemed. Rather than risk being proved wrong, even by themselves, their minds instead distracted them with a remarkable number of thoughts (such as 'I like the experimenter!') that were safely irrelevant to the task in hand.

Twisting information and self-censoring arguments – strategies we unconsciously use to keep the balance of evidence weighing more heavily on our own side of the scales – keep us buoyantly self-assured. And what is more, the faith we hold in the infallibility of our beliefs is so powerful that we are even capable of *creating* evidence to prove ourselves right – the self-fulfilling prophecy. The placebo effect – in which a fake treatment somehow makes you better simply because you think you are receiving an effective remedy for your complaint – is probably the best-known example of this.[9] And when a genuine treatment doesn't enjoy the benefit of the brain's high hopes for it, it becomes remarkably less effective. When you toss down a few painkillers, it is in no small way your confidence that the drug will relieve your headache that makes the pain go away. A group of patients recovering from lung surgery were told by their doctor that they would be given morphine intravenously for the pain.[10] Within an hour of the potent painkiller entering their bloodstream their pain intensity ratings had halved. A second group of post-surgery patients were given exactly the same dose of morphine via their drip, but weren't told about it. An hour later, these uninformed patients' ratings of the intensity of the pain had reduced only half as much as in the other group. However, ignorance was bliss (relatively speaking) in a second experiment in which the intravenous morphine was withdrawn. Patients not told that their supply of pain relief had been interrupted remained comfortable for longer than patients who had been apprised of the change in drug regimen. Even ten hours later, twice as many uninformed patients were still willing to battle on with the pain without requesting more relief.

Even more extraordinary are the influences that other people's beliefs can have on you. Psychologists first of all directed their interest in the self-fulfilling prophecy upon themselves. Could a psychologist be unwittingly encouraging her volunteers to act in line with her beliefs about what should happen in the experiment? Psychologists found that they did indeed have this strange power over their experimentees.[11] Exactly the same experimental set-up reliably yields different results, depending on the beliefs of the researcher who is running the experiment and interacting with the participants. (In fact, even rats are susceptible to the expectations of experimenters.) Researchers can also unknowingly affect the health of participants in clinical drug trials. In a twist on the placebo effect, the *researcher's* beliefs about the effectiveness of a drug influence how effective it actually is. For this very reason, good clinical trials of drugs are now run double-blind. Neither the patient nor the researcher knows what treatment the patient is getting.

Psychologists then got curious about whether the self-fulfilling prophecy might be silently at work outside the lab in the real world. In a notorious experiment, two psychologists, Robert Rosenthal and Lenore Jacobsen, turned their attention to the school classroom.[12] They gave a group of schoolchildren a fake test, which they claimed was a measure of intellectual potential. Then, supposedly on the basis of the test results, they told teachers that little Johnny, Eddy, Sally and Mary would be displaying an intellectual blossoming over the next few months. In fact, these children had been plucked randomly from the class list. Yet the teachers' mere expectation that these children would shortly be unfurling their mental wings actually led to a real and measurable enhancement of their intelligence. Teachers 'teach more and teach it more warmly' to students of whom they have great expectations, concludes Rosenthal. It's extraordinary to consider what a powerful impact a teacher's particular prejudices and stereotypes must have on your child. And the prophecy is not only self-fulfilling, it's self-perpetuating as well. When your son unwittingly fulfils his teacher's belief that 'boys don't like reading', that belief will become yet more comfortably established in the teacher's mind.

There is something really very eerie about the power of other people's beliefs to control you without your knowledge. But there is little you can do to protect yourself against an enemy whose potency resides in its very imperceptibility. But even creepier, surely, is the prospect that your own pessimistic convictions could be insidiously working against *you*. A woman's expectations for how her relationship will turn out, for example, may 'create her own reality'.[13] If she were excessively concerned about a romantic partner's true commitment to the relationship and overly preoccupied with the possibility of rejection by him, could a woman's hypersensitive reactions to conflict in her relationship bring about the very outcome she feared? In a test of this hypothesis, psychologists invited couples to place the dynamics of their relationship under microscopic scrutiny. Both members of each couple separately rated their feelings about their partner and their relationship, their satisfaction with it and their commitment. They also filled out a questionnaire that probed for anxieties about rejection from 'significant others' before they were brought together again and seated in a room with a video camera pointed at them. Next, to create a little interesting conflict, they were asked to discuss an issue in their relationship that tended to chill atmospheres and fray tempers. Then – just to see what effect this rattling of each other's cages had had – they once again separately rated their emotions about their loved one. Once they had both safely departed from the laboratory, other psychologists (who did not know what the experiment was about) did what we all wish we could do as we rake through the ashes of a scorching argument. They reran the tape to comb for unambiguous evidence of scratchy comments, nasty put-downs, hostile gestures, or unpleasant tones of voice.

Before the videotaped discussions, the partners of rejection-sensitive women were just as positive about their relationship as the partners of women with a more robust attitude towards relationships. But afterwards, the partners of the touchier women were quietly fuming. The researchers discovered the reason for this in the videotapes. The women who feared rejection behaved more cantankerously during the airing of conflict-ridden issues and, according to the researchers' statistical analyses, it was this that was so exasperating their partners. Enough to dissolve the relationship? It seemed so. A second experiment showed that the relationships of rejection-sensitive women – despite being just as healthy and happy to begin with – were nearly three times more likely to end than those of women who took conflict in their stride. Expecting rejection, these more vulnerable women behaved in ways that turned their fears into reality.

So far, our reluctance to survey the world with an open mind seems to have little to recommend it. Are there any potential benefits to be had from our obduracy? Psychologists have pointed out that a modicum of obstinacy in relinquishing our beliefs is only sensible. After all, we would end up in rather a flap if our beliefs were forever fluctuating in response to every newspaper report or argument with an in-law. There's also a sense in which our important beliefs are an integral part of who we are. To bid a belief adieu is to lose a cherished portion of our identity.[14] Interestingly, people who have recently indulged in extensive contemplation of their best qualities (or been 'self-affirmed', to use the cloying terminology of the literature) are more receptive to arguments that challenge their strongly held beliefs about issues like capital punishment and abortion. By hyping up an important area of self-worth, you are better able to loosen your grip on some of your defining values. (Just loosen your grip, mind. Not actually let go.) It's a curious, and somewhat disquieting, fact that effusive flattery dulls the sword of an intellectual opponent far more effectively than mere logical argument.

It would be much more pleasant to leave it at that: we're pig-headed, yes, but it's for good reasons. However, research shows that our stubbornness is so pernicious that even the most ground-less and fledgling belief enjoys secure residence in our brains. As a consequence, we are at the mercy of our initial opinions and impressions. In a classic demonstration of this, some volunteers were given a test of their social sensitivity.[15] They read a series of pairs of suicide notes and for each pair they had to guess which note was genuine and which was a fake. Some volunteers were then arbitrarily told that their social-sensitivity performance was superior, others that it was inferior. A little later the experimenter debriefed the volunteers. The experimenter explained that the feedback they'd been given about their social sensitivity was made up, and that their supposed score had been randomly decided before they even walked into the lab. Any ideas the volunteers had developed about their proficiency in discriminating between genuine and fake suicide notes should have been abolished by the debriefing. After all, the evidence on which those beliefs were based had been entirely discredited. But still, the volunteers con-tinued to believe in their superior or inferior social sensitivity. When the experimenter asked the volunteers to guess how well they would actually do on this and other similar tasks, their answers reflected whether they had been given 'superior per-formance' or 'inferior performance' false feedback on the suicide notes task. What is particularly remarkable about this experiment is that even people who were told that they were social clodhoppers carried on believing it. Even though their vain brains had been handed a bona fide rationale on which to restore their self-esteem, they continued to believe the worst about themselves.

In a similar experiment, researchers gave high school students training in how to solve a difficult mathematical problem.[16] Half of the students watched a clear and helpful video presentation. The other half watched a deliberately confusing video presentation that left them floundering. Unsurprisingly, these latter students wound up feeling pretty crestfallen over their ham-handedness with numbers. This lack of confidence persisted even after the researchers showed them the clear video presentation and explained that their poor maths performance was due to the bad instruction, not to their actual ability. Even three weeks later, the students unfortunate enough to have watched the baffling video presentation were less likely to show interest in signing up for other similar maths classes. And so, possibly, the entire course of their future lives was changed.

Indeed, at this point you may be beginning to feel uneasy stirrings about the ethics of psychology researchers giving false feedback – particularly negative feedback – to unsuspecting volunteers. The first chapter of this book, 'The Vain Brain', bulged with experiments in which unsuspecting volunteers were told something unpleasant about their personalities, skills, future prospects or health. To be sure, the experimenters always debriefed the hapless volunteers afterwards, but it looks as if this alone isn't enough. The researchers in the suicide notes experiment discovered that normal debriefing procedures are hopelessly ineffective in correcting pigheadedly held beliefs. Only by painstakingly explaining the belief-perseverance phenomenon, and describing how it might affect the volunteer, were the experimenters able to leave their volunteers in the same psychological condition in which they found them.

This is a little worrisome – although evidently not to psychology researchers. Of course, you can see it from a researcher's point of view. Yes, you tell some helpful person who has kindly agreed to help you in your research that, oh dear, he's scored embarrassingly low on a test compared with almost everyone else who's ever passed through the lab. But then, probably less than an hour later, you clearly explain that what you told him wasn't true, that you didn't even trouble to mark his test. It's hard to credit that this might be insufficient to rid even the most self-doubting individual of any lingering doubts.

Clearly, however, normal debriefing *is* strangely inadequate. Why is it that beliefs take such an immediate and tenacious grasp of our brains? One answer is that our rich, imaginative and generally spurious explanations of things are to blame. You hear a rumour that a friend's teenager is pregnant. Discussing her dubious situation with another friend, you sadly call attention to the parents' regrettable insistence on treating adolescents as if they were adults, the laissez-faire attitude of the mother towards curfews, and the risqué clothes in which they let their daughter appear in public. In the face of such parental licence, the young woman's predicament takes on a tragic inevitability. As a result, when you subsequently learn that the rumoured pregnancy concerned someone else's daughter, you find yourself thinking that it is only a matter of time before the slandered girl suffers the same misfortune. You may even comment, with the satisfying (if, in your case, misguided) confidence of Cassandra, that, 'There's no smoke without fire.' The initial belief recruits its own web of supporting evidence, derived from the facile causal explanations that we're so good at creating (and which, let's be honest, are so much fun to indulge in). You can then take the initial fact away. The web of explanation is strong enough to support the belief without it.

In an experiment that simulated just this kind of gossipy social reasoning, volunteers were given a real clinical case history to read.[17] One case study, 'Shirley K.', was an anxious young mother and housewife whose history included such misfortunes as divorce, the suicide of her lover, her father's death, and the eventual commitment of her mother to a mental institution. Some of the volunteers were then asked to put themselves in the role of a clinical psychologist who had just learned that Shirley K. had subsequently committed suicide. They were asked what clues, if any, they found in Shirley K.'s life story that might help a psychologist explain or predict her suicide. The volunteers embraced this task with enthusiasm. They easily came up with plausible-sounding hypotheses; for example, that the suicide of her lover was 'a model that led her to take her own life'. Once the volunteers had done this they were told that in fact nothing was known about Shirley K.'s future life. The suicide they had been asked to explain was only hypothetical. However, the web of explanation had been spun. When asked how likely it was that Shirley K.

would in fact commit suicide, the volunteers rated this as being much more likely than did another group of people who had not been asked to explain the hypothetical suicide. In fact, even people told beforehand that the suicide didn't actually happen nonetheless found their theories about why a suicide *might* have occurred so convincing that they, too, pegged Shirley K. as a high suicide risk.

A later study showed just how crucial these sorts of speculations are in helping to bolster a belief. In a variation of the experiment in which volunteers were given made-up information about their ability to tell the difference between genuine and fake suicide notes, volunteers were told (as in the original experiment) that their performance was either superior or inferior. As before, some of the volunteers were then left free to run wild with theories to explain their supposed level of social sensitivity. When later told that the feedback they had been given had been fabricated, they nonetheless continued to cling to their newfound belief about their social abilities (just as did the volunteers in the original experiment). The false feedback they had received was by then just a small part of the 'evidence' they had for their opinion regarding their social sensitivity. Something very different happened, however, with a second group of volunteers who were prevented from searching for explanations for their allegedly good or bad performance on the task. These volunteers were immediately commanded to keep themselves busy in an absorbing task. Denied the opportunity to rummage in their brains for other evidence to support their flimsy belief about their social sensitivity, they sensibly abandoned the belief as soon as they learnt that it was based on lies. It's our irresistible urge to play amateur psychologist that makes us so vulnerable to our initial beliefs, no matter how bluntly the facts they were based on may be discredited. It's human nature to try to explain everything that happens around us, perhaps as a way to make life seem less capricious.

Our susceptibility to first impressions is compounded by another, rather endearing, human failing. We are credulous creatures who find it easy to believe, but difficult to doubt. The problem is that we believe things to be true as a matter of course. As psychologist Daniel Gilbert has put it, 'you can't not believe everything you read'.[18] Of course, we are not lumbered with our gullible beliefs forever, or even for very long. However, it is only with some mental effort that we can decide that they are untrue. Our natural urge – our default position – is to believe. This may be because, in general, people speak the truth more often than not. It's therefore more efficient to assume that things are true unless we have reason to think otherwise.

But there is a problem with this system. If your brain is too busy with other things to put in the necessary legwork to reject a porkie pie, then you're stuck with that belief. Advertisers and car salesmen will be delighted to learn that incredulity really is hard work for us, or so research suggests. If your brain is distracted or under pressure, you will tend to believe statements that you would normally find rather dubious.[19] In fact, you may even find yourself believing things you were explicitly told were untrue. In one demonstration of this failure to 'unbelieve', volunteers read from a computer screen a series of statements about a criminal defendant (for example, 'The robber had a gun').[20] Some of the statements were false. The volunteers knew exactly which ones they were, because they appeared in a different colour of text. For some of the volunteers, the untrue statements they were shown were designed to make the crime seem more heinous. For others, the false testimony made the crime seem more forgivable. At the same time that the volunteers were reading the statements, a string of digits also marched across the computer screen. Some of the volunteers had to push a button whenever they saw the digit '5'. Banal though this may seem, doing this uses up quite a lot of mental resources. This meant that these volunteers had less brainpower available to mentally switch the labelling of the false statements from the default 'true' to 'false'. These busy volunteers were much more likely to misremember false statements as true. What's more, this affected how long they thought the criminal should serve in prison. When the false statements unfairly exacerbated the severity of the crime, the distracted volunteers sentenced him to prison for almost twice as long a stretch.

Indeed, if your reputation is under examination, the gullible brains of others can put you in serious jeopardy. Because of our bias towards belief, we are particularly susceptible to innuendo. In a simulation of media election coverage, volunteers read a series of headlines about political candidates, and then gave their impressions of each of the politicians.[21] Unsurprisingly, headlines such as 'BOB TALBERT ASSOCIATED WITH FRAUDULENT CHARITY' left Talbert's reputation in tatters. Astonishingly, though, the headline 'IS BOB TALBERT ASSOCIATED WITH FRAUDULENT CHARITY?' was just as damaging. And if you're thinking of entering the public eye yourself, consider this: even

the headline 'BOB TALBERT NOT LINKED WITH FRAUDU-
LENT CHARITY' was incriminating in the eyes of the readers.
Denials are, after all, nothing more than statements with a
'not' tagged on. The bit about 'Bob Talbert' and 'fraudulent
charity' slips into our brains easily enough, but the 'not' isn't
somehow quite as effective as it should be in affecting our beliefs.[22]
We are suckers for innuendo, even – as the study went on to show
– when it comes from a disreputable source like a tabloid.
Though we all think ourselves immune to it, negative campaign-
ing works.

For any defendant under scrutiny in the courtroom, the
beliefs of gullible brains are, of course, of crucial significance.
Remember the joke circulating prior to the O. J. Simpson trial?

Knock, knock.

Who's there?

O.J.

O.J. who?

You're on the jury.

Pre-trial publicity is usually very bad news for a defendant whose
future liberty or even life depends on the machinations of twelve
pigheaded brains.[23] Perhaps because of our susceptibility to
innuendo and even denials, media reports of crime encourage a
pro-prosecution stance in jurors. It has been shown that the more
people know about a case before the trial, the more guilty they
think the defendant. And grisly media coverage aggravates the

lock-him-up attitude even further, even though the brutality of a crime obviously has no bearing whatsoever on whether that particular defendant is guilty. A juror who wallows in pre-trial publicity skews Justice's scales against the defendant, and the pig-headed brain that then biases, distorts and even makes up evidence to support this belief in the defendant's guilt certainly won't help to restore the balance.

And it is not just jurors who should be on their guard. Prurient spectators, too, of high-publicity trials are persuaded into complacent self-assurance. Looking back on the trial from a post-verdict vantage point, the brain implacably refuses to concede that its predictive powers were ever anything less than perfect. 'I knew it all along', you tell yourself, surreptitiously adjusting memory. With the benefit of hindsight, what has happened seems inevitable and foreseeable – and you convince yourself that foresee it you did. Amid the scandal of the Bill Clinton impeachment trial, researchers interested in the hindsight-bias phenomenon asked people to estimate, at periods of both three weeks and three days before the much anticipated verdict, how likely it was that Clinton would be convicted.[24] The media reports during this period made it seem increasingly likely that Clinton would be let off the hook, and the respondents' speculations over that time as to his chances did change accordingly. No more than four days after the verdict, these people humbly and correctly remembered that their opinion had shifted over time towards the correct view that Clinton would be acquitted. But just a week after that, they were brashly claiming that they'd been pretty sure all along that Clinton wouldn't be convicted. (They also believed that they, and they alone, enjoyed these powers of early prophecy. Asked about the speculations of the average American, or their best friend, they judged that these inferior beings were slower to read the runes than they themselves had been.)

Even when researchers explicitly command people to answer as if they don't know about things that have actually happened, or firmly warn them of our propensity to exaggerate how much we would have guessed anyhow, we continue to deny that the knowledge to which we are privy has influenced us, and insist we would have known it all along.[25] Our refusal to acknowledge that our opinions benefit from hindsight is particularly troublesome for legal cases in which jurors decide whether to award punitive damages. (Punitive damages essentially say to the defendant, 'Naughty! Should have seen that one coming.') In a simulation of this sort of case, people were given testimony about an actual accident in which a Southern Pacific train had derailed, spilling toxic herbicide into the Sacramento River in California.[26] Some volunteers were told only that the National Transportation Safety Board, reckoning the track to be hazardous, had slapped an order on the railway to stop operations, and that the railroad wanted the order lifted. They were shown extensive expert testimony about the various defects and dangers of the condition of the train and its mountainous track as it was just before the real accident none of them knew about. They were then asked to decide whether the risk of an accident was such that the order should stay in place. Totally unaware of what had actually happened on this stretch of railroad, these mock jurors proved fairly optimistic about the safety of the track. Only a third of them thought that the hazards were serious enough to justify stopping the train from running.

Contrast this with the views of the other volunteers, who were able to inspect the details of the case through the crystal clear lens of hindsight. These volunteers were told both of the derailment and the consequent pollution of the river. They then viewed exactly the same expert testimony as the other group of volunteers. Before the accident occurred, they were asked, was there a grave danger or risk of harm that was a foreseeable and likely consequence of the condition of the tracks? Knowing that such harm had indeed occurred, and unable to perform the mental gymnastics necessary to pretend they didn't, two-thirds of the volunteers said yes, an accident was likely and the railroad should have realised this. In their view, punitive damages should be awarded. The difference in the outlooks offered by foresight and hindsight suggests that, once an accident has happened, our assessment of responsibility can become unreasonably high.

We have seen how the brain pretends to know what it did not or would not have known. But things don't stop there. The brain also lays claim to knowledge of what it cannot know. As a final embarrassment in this sorry catalogue of our cocky tendencies, we think we know what (if we only knew it) can't be known at all. So omniscient does the pigheaded brain think itself that it even affects to be acquainted with knowledge that doesn't exist. University student volunteers were given a hundred general knowledge questions to answer.[27] Sneakily scattered among them, however, were twenty questions to which there was no answer (such as, 'What is the name of the only type of cat native to

Australia?', 'What is the name of the legendary floating island in ancient Greece?' or 'What is the last name of the only woman to sign the Declaration of Independence?'). On about 20 per cent of these unanswerable questions the volunteers claimed to be on the verge of dredging up the answer. They *knew* it was in there somewhere. It was on the tip of their tongue!

Blinded by our own brilliance, we think we know it all.

The ramifications of our pigheadedness spread far wider than controversy over the correct method for decanting spaghetti. Beyond the dramas of the kitchen sink, our complacent obstinacy rears its ugly head everywhere: it's in the bedroom, the classroom, the social scene, the scientist's laboratory, the political stage, the courtroom. Pervading, as it does, every aspect of our lives, is there anything we can do to lessen the shameful and often dangerous effects of our stubbornness and conceit? At this point, psychology texts like to make a few half-hearted suggestions as to how we can combat the mulish tendencies of our minds. 'Entertain alternative hypotheses', we are urged. 'Consider the counter-evidence.' The problem, of course, is that we are convinced that we are already doing this; it's simply that the other guy's view is absurd, his arguments laughably flimsy. Our pigheadedness appears to be irredeemable. It is a sad fact that the research bears out the newspaper columnist Richard Cohen, who wrote that 'The ability to kill or capture a man is a relatively simple task compared with changing his mind.'[28]

My husband would do well to bear that in mind, come dinnertime.

CHAPTER 6

The Secretive Brain

Exposing the guile of the mental butler

I remember my husband waking up one morning exclaiming, 'I had a dream last night!' This was quite an event, since my husband generally claims not to dream. He clearly expected me to show an interest: if not professionally, then at least in my role as spouse. Certainly, as a psychologist – indoctrinated to value only strictly scientific methods – I was entirely unequipped to offer my husband a Freudian analysis of his slumberous labours. The name Freud was not one mentioned often in the psychology department I attended as an undergraduate. Indeed, it was rumoured that his dusty collected works on the library shelves were wired to a generator. Anyone misguided enough to touch them would receive an enlightening electric shock – that popular educational tool of the experimental psychologist. Yet although I stand firmly in the camp of those who think 'Penis envy? Puh-*lease*', there is something tantalising about the promise offered by dreams, to reveal the secret machinations that go on below the paper-thin surface of the conscious mind. Which is why, despite myself, I felt a little thrill of excitement in response to my husband's announcement. Here at last was an unprecedented opportunity to take a peek at the uncensored ruminations of my husband's hidden mind. Thus it was that I found myself asking him to tell me all about his dream.

'I dreamed that we had an argument', he said proudly.

'Interesting', I replied thoughtfully. 'We had an argument last night.'

'Yes, my dream was almost exactly the same. God, I was mad. Do you want some tea?'

And there ended my brief psychoanalytic journey of discovery into my spouse's unconscious mind.

Fortunately, psychoanalysis is no longer the only route available into the covert portion of our mind. Over the past few decades social psychologists have been getting very interested in this aspect of our mental life, and what it's up to. Their research shows that there's both good news and bad news. The good news is that the unconscious isn't, as it's often billed, merely the boxing ring for psychic struggles. The unconscious mind works hard, efficiently and tirelessly on your behalf. One prominent social psychologist refers to it as the 'mental butler' who tends silently to our needs and desires, without us even having to trouble to ring the bell.[1] With the grunt work covered, the conscious mind is left at leisure to ponder life goals, make important decisions and generally run the show.

Or *does* it? The bad news is that delegation always comes at a cost to control. When you hand over a job to your willing unconscious, you can never be quite sure how it's being done.

Actually, that's not the bad news. I just didn't want to break it to you too suddenly, while you were still glorying in the metaphor of your conscious self as master of the manor lording it over your staff of unconscious mental processes. The real bad news is that even our relatively rare moments of conscious choice may be nothing but an illusion. Like the hapless toff Bertie Wooster, who is but putty in the hands of his scheming butler Jeeves, recent research suggests that the hand that polishes the shoes walks the feet. You only *think* you're in charge of where you're going.

However, the unconscious – like Jeeves – is as indispensable as it is devious. Everyday activities, like walking and driving, perfectly illustrate the importance of being able to delegate responsibility to the unconscious mind. This point was vividly brought home to me as I observed my toddler son learning how to walk. When he was twelve months old it was an activity requiring the utmost concentration. No other business – receiving a proffered toy, taking a sip of water, even surveying the pathway ahead for obstacles – could be conducted at the same time. Imagine if this carried on throughout life, with passers-by on the street plopping clumsily to their bottoms should you distract them for an instant by asking for directions. But fortunately, the unconscious gradually takes over. The previously tricky aspects of walking – balancing upright, moving forward, the whole left-foot–right-foot routine – become automatic and mentally effortless. And once a skill moves into the domain of the unconscious mind, we free up our conscious thought for other matters. The learner driver is a poor conversationalist because his conscious mind is fully taken up with the complexities of steering, changing gears and indicating. As driving becomes automatic, we can offer something a little more fulfilling to our front-seat companion than a series of fractured mutterings and muffled cries of 'Sorry!' Precious conscious thought becomes available again.

And conscious thought *is* precious. Famously a stream, rather than tributary, of consciousness, it limits you to just a single line of inner dialogue at any one time. So since there's only one of the conscious you, you need droves of full-time help from the mental downstairs. Of course, there's nothing particularly secretive or sinister about the idea of the conscious will demanding 'Home, James' and the unconscious following the order by smoothly taking over the routine of driving. But what if the unconscious could itself trigger the very act of willing, setting itself off in the pursuit of a goal without a conscious command from above?[2] Recent research has caught the unconscious in this very act. If you're an experienced driver, a curve in the road triggers the unconscious to adjust the steering wheel without you even having to think about it. You might see the curve, but you don't notice the automatic effect it has on your steering. In a similar way, as we become experienced navigators of the social highway, the people and situations we encounter automatically trigger our unconscious to adjust our social steering in line with well-practised goals, without us even realising.

Because our relationships with others are such hotbeds of motivations and goals, our unconscious is particularly easily sparked off in this way by people. And since no chapter on the unconscious, however modern in its approach, would be complete without mention of mothers, we will take the worthy aim of 'making mother proud' as an example of an 'interpersonal goal'. If this is one of your goals (and I certainly hope it is) then your unconscious will not have failed to notice that when you find yourself thinking 'But what would mother say?' you strive to be and do better. So what the helpful unconscious does is to automatically set you the goal of going that extra mile, whenever anything in your situation reminds it of your mother. You, in the meantime – the conscious you, that is – are completely unaware that you're acting under the influence of a hidden agenda.

In a demonstration of this, researchers recruited volunteer students who – months and months before – had been asked to write down the sorts of goals they had with respect to their mothers.[3] The volunteers were chosen so that about equal numbers did and did not have the goal of making their mother proud.

The researchers then poked the unconscious into automatically activating mother-related goals in some of the volunteers. They did this by priming the mother schema, to use the technical terms. Schemas make up the filing system of your mind. Cognitive psychologists think that just about everything we learn about the world is neatly tidied away into a schema. I like to think of a schema as a big bed full of slumbering brain cells. All the brain cells in the bed represent a different part of the schema. So, for example, in the schema for dogs you'll find brain cells that – when active and awake – point out that dogs have four legs. Then there are the neurons that hold the information that dogs bark, neurons that remind you that dogs have hair, and all the neurons for just about everything else you know about the concept of dogs. And they're all tucked up in the same bed.

Priming a schema is like shaking a few of the brain cells awake. Because they're all snuggled up cosily, waking one group of brain cells disturbs the sleep of all the others in the bed, and makes them more likely to wake up. And brain cells that are on the verge of wakefulness are much more likely to answer the call of the conscious than are brain cells sleeping undisturbed in some other schema bed. (For example, researchers primed the Asian schema in some volunteers by using an Asian experimenter to present a word-completion task.[4] For the other volunteers, the experimenter was white. The task was to make words from fragments such as 'POLI_E' and 'S_Y'. The volunteers whose Asian schemas were primed were more likely to come up with words from the Asian schema, like 'POLITE' and 'SHY', rather than, say, 'POLICE' and 'SKY'.)

To return to our make-mother-proud experiment, the researchers primed the mother schema in some of the volunteers by asking them several questions about their mother: how old she was when she got married, her hobbies, political preferences and so on. In other words, they shook awake all the brain cells involved with information about 'MOTHER: MAJOR LIFE EVENTS, INTERESTS AND VALUES'. The researchers knew that this would also disturb the brain cells concerned with 'MOTHER: GOALS PERTAINING TO', which would all be lying somewhere in the same bed. The unprimed volunteers were instead asked questions about themselves; their mother schema remained untouched. Next, all the volunteers were asked to try a verbal-skills task, which involved generating as many words as they could in five minutes from a set of seven letters. How the volunteers did on the task depended both on whether they had the goal to make mother proud, and whether their mother schemas were primed. Volunteers who wanted to make their mother proud *and* had had their mother schema activated outperformed all of the other groups.

Don't think, however, that these volunteers were consciously thinking, 'I must do well so I can tell Mum about this and make her proud of me.' The volunteers were quizzed carefully afterwards, and none realised that answering questions about their mother might have influenced how they did on the verbal-skills task. Rather, it was the helpful unconscious that – while shaking part of the mother schema awake in the first part of the experiment – had also jostled the goal of making mother proud into action, influencing how hard the volunteer worked on the word-generating task.

Indeed, proof that the unconscious truly acts off its own bat (and not in response to conscious decisions to try harder) comes from priming experiments in which conscious awareness is bypassed altogether. In subliminal priming, a picture or word (for example, the word 'mother') is flashed up too briefly for you to become consciously aware of it, but long enough so that the quicker unconscious notices it. (About one tenth to one half of a second does the trick.) Subliminally priming volunteers has just the same sort of effect as the priming in the make-mother-proud experiment. For example, some volunteers were subliminally primed with the word 'father' before an analytic reasoning test.[5] Afterwards, they were asked if it was important to their father that they, the volunteer, be a good analytic reasoner. Among the volunteers who said yes, it made a big difference whether or not they had been subliminally flashed with the word 'father' before the reasoning test. Father-primed volunteers significantly outdid their unprimed peers. Although they were completely oblivious to the surreptitious paternal flickering, it still had the power to make them work harder on the task.

What these and many other similar experiments show is that seemingly trivial things in our environment may be influencing our behaviour. Dormant goals are triggered without our even realising. It's not that we're necessarily unaware of the stimulus itself. However, we are oblivious to the effect that it is having on us. Without our knowledge, we suddenly begin to pursue a goal that has been set off by some seemingly innocuous event. For example, if someone asks you about a good friend and then asks you for a favour, you will be more willing to help. This is because thinking about friends unconsciously primes the goal to help, so one experiment found.[6] Seemingly incidental events and objects appear to have dark powers over our behaviour, and the speculation begins where the experiments stop. Is that charming photo of your family on the desk at work imperceptibly encouraging you to head home earlier? If you have a deadline coming up, should you replace the family photo with a portrait of your boss instead? What about that stapler; what's it up to? Looks innocent enough, but who knows what riot of motives it may be stirring in your brain.

OK, the stapler is probably guiltless. But there are countless other suspects (the letter from your mother on the doormat, the song you heard on the radio on the way to work, maybe even that dead pigeon on the pavement), all of which may be changing the course of your life in their own, modest little way. And the unconscious doesn't stop at the willy-nilly firing up of goals, which are at least motives to which you knowingly subscribe. Any sort of schema can be primed. And when it is, our behaviour changes to fit with it. In one of the first extraordinary demonstrations of this phenomenon, volunteers had to unscramble several sentences in which the words were in the wrong order.[7] For some of the volunteers, the sentences used words related to the stereotype of old people: 'wrinkle', 'bitter', 'knits', 'forgetful', 'stubborn', and so on. The rest of the volunteers unscrambled sentences with only neutral words. The point of this was to prime the elderly schema in the first group of volunteers, and to see what effect this had on their behaviour. So once each volunteer had finished the task and gathered their belongings, the researcher thanked them, showed them to the door and pointed out the lift at the end of the hall. But the experiment was not yet over: a confederate lurking in the hallway then secretly timed how long the volunteer took to walk down the corridor. Those who had re-arranged words related to old people actually behaved like stooped old frost-tops themselves on the journey to the lift, walking significantly more slowly than the other volunteers.

As you might imagine, this generous propensity of your unconscious to invite any old schema knocking on the back door to come on in and join the party can be a good thing or a bad thing. It all depends on the schema. Volunteers primed with the schema of professors – a supposedly intelligent and knowledgeable breed – stormed their way to success at Trivial Pursuit, compared with others not so benefited.[8] But prime people instead with the football hooligan schema, and what ensues is Trivial

Pursuit meltdown. Dust off the polite schema in people's brains, and the majority will wait patiently for more than ten minutes without interrupting the experimenter's mundane conversation with another student. Kindle the rudeness schema instead, and most people will butt in long before ten minutes have passed.[9]

As if this mental mayhem weren't already enough to contemplate, do we also need to worry about our promiscuous unconscious being wooed by shameless subliminal marketing campaigns? Many people have heard of the nefarious début of subliminal priming made in the world of advertising back in the 1950s. James Vicary, the executive of a failing advertising company, claimed to have sky-rocketed coke and popcorn sales at cinemas by subliminally flashing 'DRINK COKE' and 'EAT POP-CORN' messages at unsuspecting cinema-goers. It turned out to be a hoax – there had been no secret messages. Vicary was right not to have bothered: subliminal advertising didn't actually seem to have any real effects on people's attitudes towards products, or their buying behaviour.[10]

However, advertisers hadn't then fully mastered the tricky technical side of successful subliminal priming (for example, you need many flashes of the prime rather than just a few, and single words work better than sentences).[11] These days, social psychologists are becoming disturbingly successful at catching the 'consumer unconscious'. Using up-to-date priming techniques, they can influence people's attitudes towards advertised products. Volunteers subliminally flashed with a happy face before being offered a fruit-flavoured drink rated the concoction tastier, drank more of it and were even willing to pay double the price for it, compared with volunteers flashed with angry faces.[12] In another experiment, volunteers subliminally primed with words to do with thirst thought that the thirst-quenching 'SuperQuencher' drink sounded superior to the energy-giving 'PowerPro' beverage. They also drank more of it, compared with volunteers not primed in this way.[13] However, in both experiments the volunteers had to be thirsty in order for the priming to work. Priming had no effect at all on volunteers who came pre-quenched. Will this be our best defence, then, when the new wave of underhanded advertising begins – to be sure to visit the movies only when sated and slaked to the gills? Sadly, even this may not protect us. People shown a very special episode of *The Simpsons* didn't realise that twenty-four subliminal flashes of Coca-Cola cans and the boxer Sugar Ray Leonard (gleaming with sweat and looking much in need of a long cool drink) had been carefully inserted between the frames. Yet afterwards, they felt strangely thirsty . . .[14]

Part of the reason why advertisers can so easily sully your opinions with their grubby fingers is that the taciturn unconscious prefers to leave you in the dark about so many things. Rather than interrupt your important ruminations about what you'd like to drink with your lunch, it quietly gets on with the business of helping you to make the decision. Then, loathe to disturb your enjoyment of the chosen beverage, it doesn't trouble to tell you that a smiling face, flashed too fast for the plodding conscious you to notice, is actually the reason you chose a fruit cordial of such doubtful horticultural origin. Because of this reluctance on the part of our secretive brain to speak up, we often have no great insight into the mysterious cog-turnings from which our opinions spring. But, control-freaks as we are, we do feel the need to cling to the illusion that we know what is going on. To maintain this pleasing self-deception, we have to take on the role of detective and search for clues that will explain our feelings. Unfortunately, though, when the location of the evidence isn't signalled with a large X to mark the spot, our talent for sleuthing is revealed to be somewhat lacking. Oblivious to the true facts, we're easily distracted by red herrings. Weaving a theory around them, our conjectures may enjoy the veneer of plausibility, but they are sadly mistaken.

In everyday life, even though all of your neighbours may have to stifle their sniggers when you offer your own explanation of exactly why it was, one week before your fiftieth birthday, you rushed out and bought that sleek new powerful sports car, not even the most experienced therapist can prove you wrong. Within the stripped-down confines of the psychology laboratory, however, you are far less safe. Here, it is simple to embarrass the brain in its brash postulations. In one such experiment, psychologists asked volunteers to predict in which of three boxes on a computer screen a red circle would appear.[15] Following each guess, the selected box revealed either a red or a black circle, superimposed on an abstract pattern. Whenever the volunteers happened to choose the box with the red circle they were given a chocolate to eat and – congratulating themselves on how very clever they had been at intuiting yet another little red dot's movements – they would joyfully gobble it down. Unbeknown to them, however, whether or not their guesses were correct was predetermined, and the experiment was about something else altogether. It had been designed so that the red circle usually appeared on one particular, if unrecognisable, doodle, whereas the black circle usually appeared on a different one. What the researchers were really interested in was whether the volunteers would, after the experiment was over, think that the abstract squiggle that appeared with the red circle (and the sweet) was aesthetically superior to the picture that appeared with the unrewarded black circle, and to other, previously unseen, meaningless sketches.

So, pretending that the important bit of the experiment was over, the experimenter asked the volunteers if they'd mind offering their opinions on the attractiveness of some pictures. The pile they were given included the patterns they had already seen. To an unbiased brain there really wasn't anything between them, but the volunteers – the taste of chocolate still lingering on their lips – revealed a penchant for whichever picture had been discreetly placed beneath the red dots. To us, it is obvious why. Like Pavlov's dogs, who salivated at the sound of the bell that signalled the arrival of dinner, the volunteers associated the pattern with the taste satisfaction of confection. But they didn't realise this. In fact, careful questioning revealed that they hadn't even noticed they'd seen the patterns before. This did not stop them, however, from coming up with explanations as to why they preferred one picture over another. Searching for an answer in the meaningless tangle of lines, the volunteers came up with impressively credible-sounding reasons for their preferences. The picture's superiority, they confidently claimed, derived from its similarity to the counterpane in their grandmother's house, for example, or its resemblance to the ocean in Florida. Were they not the victim of a cunningly designed, cold-blooded experiment, there would be no reason on earth to doubt their word. As it is, like the neighbours of the new owner of both a midlife crisis and a splendid new car, we chuckle behind our hands at the poor sap's humiliating lack of insight.

As experiments of this sort so mercilessly reveal, our fumbling efforts at detection are more Clouseau than Poirot. As we attempt to understand ourselves, our speculations as to why we are feeling what we are feeling can carry us way off course. Remember the Stanford students described in 'The Deluded Brain' who, under hypnotic suggestion, felt unusually aroused but couldn't recall the reason for it?[16] The ideas they came up with to explain their unexpected sensations were not only wrong, they bordered on the pathological.

And it's not just our feelings that can bamboozle us this way. According to self-perception theory, the reasons behind our actual behaviour are also something of a mystery to us.[17] Lacking enlightenment, we have to perform the cumbersome task of placing ourselves on the psychiatrist's couch whenever we want to know why we did certain things. And, as we would with anyone else whose inner tickings we wished to probe, we infer our own motives from anything around us. Nursery-school children were the targets in the classic experiment exploring this seemingly improbable hypothesis.[18] Researchers, armed with felt-tip pens, descended upon these young innocents. Some of the children were told that, if they busied themselves drawing with the pens, then they'd be rewarded with both a gold star and a ribbon (two thrilling items for your average preschooler). True to this promise, after the children had scribbled away for a while, the researchers solemnly presented them with the sticker and ribbon they had earned. Other children, by contrast, were also given a selection of felt-tip pens to play with, but no particular incentive to use them.

A few days later the researchers returned to the nursery, once again equipped with the pens. This time, however, the pens were casually left lying about for the children to play with if they pleased. The researchers wanted to know which children would be most drawn to them: those who had been rewarded a few days earlier, or those whose hands remained chastely ungreased by the bribes. Any parent who has sunk to the use of corrupting acts of enticement – that is, any parent – will assume that the proud owners of the stars and ribbons would choose to play longer with the pens. That's what fits best with our practical philosophy of parenting, after all: you bribe your children into behaving the way you'd like. But in fact it was the *unrewarded* children who spent more time playing with the pens. The reason, according to self-perception theory, is this. When the children saw this optional pastime spread out on the tabletops for the second time, they had to decide whether or not they wanted to play with them. And so their brains asked themselves, 'How do I *like* drawing with felt-tip pens?' The brains of the children in the unrewarded group answered along the lines of, 'Well, I spent all that time drawing with the pens last week, so I guess I must enjoy it. I think I'll have a go at a surrealist portrait of Mum. Tra-la-la!' But the brains of the kids in the rewarded group replied, 'Dammit, not bloody pens again. I know I played with them last week, but that was only to get the star and the ribbon. Which way's the sandpit?'

These experiments, revealing as they do the cloak-and-dagger methods of the secretive brain, have unsettling implications for us all. When we reflect on major issues in our lives – why we prefer this car or that house, why we are in this particular career, or with that particular person – the answers that we come up with are just best guesses. They may have little to do with the truth.

We have learned more than a few disturbing facts about our unconscious. Nonetheless, its description as a mental butler still seems reasonably apt. Although, unasked, the unconscious takes matters into its own hands rather often, and keeps you in the dark regarding some rather weighty matters, nonetheless it is basically on your side. And, most important of all, despite these liberties taken by the unconscious, the conscious you is still more or less in charge. You think, 'I'll take a shower', and then you take a shower. You think, 'I'll go upstairs now' and lo, there you are, trotting upstairs. You think, 'I shall move my right index finger and tap it on the desk' and – tap! – your finger submits to the command. Your fingers, like all your limbs and appendages, are servants of the masterful conscious will. All day, every day, we all decide to do things which – save for interruptions or distractions – we will then do. It's obvious to the meanest intelligence that it's the conscious will that makes things happen.

But is that really the chain of command, or do we just think that it is? After all, we know that our bodies do sometimes submit to commands to which our conscious selves can't possibly lay claim. Consider the hand that flies off the hot saucepan handle before we even feel the pain, or the foot that slams on the brake before we consciously register the traffic hazard ahead. These reflexes aren't preceded by any conscious decision, and we're happy to acknowledge the role of our unconscious mind in their speedy initiation. But suppose for a moment that there's a place in our mind we know nothing about – call it the secret commander – that spends its day sending ideas to our conscious mind. 'Tell it to think "I'll tap my right index finger now"', the secret commander shouts, and off the message goes, up to the conscious. In the meantime, the neuronal grunt workers get going obeying the secret commander by arranging the finger tap itself.

From *your* point of view – knowing nothing about the secret commander – the order of proceedings seems to be:

Think 'tap finger'.
Finger taps.

To us, it seems obvious that the thought caused the action, just as a ball hitting a vase is what causes it to topple off the mantelpiece. But the actual course of events in our little imagined scenario is quite different. A mysterious unconscious process (the secret commander) caused the thought 'tap finger' and set the finger tap in motion. But because we know nothing about the mental activity that took place before we had the great idea to tap our finger, we very reasonably infer that our finger tapped because we willed it so.[19]

You might concede that this crazy idea – that our conscious

will is a misguided delusion – is logically possible. Yes, it could happen, in theory. But why on earth should we believe it? Is there any reason to think that conscious will *isn't* actually what makes things happen?

To answer this question, we have to examine the simple process of moving one's finger in more detail than you ever thought possible. In a momentous experiment by a researcher called Benjamin Libet, volunteers made spontaneous, willed finger movements.[20] This was nothing very new or exciting for the volunteers: just the same old 'think "move finger", finger moves' sequence. Libet, in the meantime, was busy taking very precise measurements. For starters, he detected finger movements the moment they happened by using a muscle movement sensor strapped to the volunteer's finger. As a matching accessory, the volunteer's head was encased in scalp electrodes that picked up brain activity. Libet found that about half a second before a person's finger moved, there was a little flurry of brain activity, called the readiness potential. From previous research Libet knew that this flurry wasn't anything to do with implementing the actual finger movement. It wasn't the mundane but necessary instructions to get that finger up in the air. (That came later, right before the movement, in the motor control area of the brain.) What Libet was seeing when the readiness potential took place was the mighty command 'Move finger' itself.

The big question for Libet was where this command came from. Was the readiness potential a bunch of brain cells firing as the decision to raise a finger came to fruition – conscious will? Or did it correspond to the clandestine activities of the secret commander? The answer was in the timing. Libet asked his volunteers to report when exactly they became aware of having the conscious urge to perform each of their finger movements. They did this by using a specially designed clock with very small time intervals. The volunteers were carefully trained to observe where the clock hand was at the moment they had the conscious urge to move.

And here's the remarkable thing. The volunteers didn't consciously experience the will to move their finger until more than a third of a second *after* the readiness potential. In other words, the unconscious was already busy preparing for the finger movement well before the idea occurred to consciousness. You might think that this was just because the volunteers were a little slow at matching their awareness of their intention to move with the position of the clock hand. But to make sure that this wasn't the case, in another series of trials Libet stimulated the volunteers' hands and asked them to report, using the same clock, when they felt the sensation. Because Libet knew precisely when their hands had been touched, he could work out the delay involved in using the clock. Even allowing, generously, for this delay, the readiness potential in Libet's main finger-tapping experiment still came well before the conscious intention.

This astonishing finding – that the brain can be busy preparing for intentions you haven't yet had – leaves us with the mysterious question of who – or what – ordered the finger to move? It couldn't have been conscious will. Was it our hypothetical secret commander?

The possibility that conscious will is an illusion challenges our sense of free will: the feeling that we are indeed masters of our destinies. It forces us to wonder if perhaps our lives are, as William James so graphically put it, nothing more than the 'dull rattling off of a chain that was forged innumerable ages ago'. And, if our so-called voluntary acts are actually the uncontrollable decisions of the secretive unconscious, how can we hold people responsible for their actions? It is irritating enough that I can't justifiably hold my husband morally responsible for the richly sonorous breathing that accompanies his strangely dreamless sleep. Does he now have a watertight excuse for *all* of his misdemeanours? ('It wasn't me, darling. It was the secret commander. I refer you to Chapter 6 of your own book.') But all is not lost. A consoling alternative, offered by Libet himself, is that conscious free will has a final veto over the unconsciously initiated intentions that come 'bubbling up' through our brains, as he puts it.[21] According to this more comforting scenario, the mental script for our familiar finger-tapping scenario could potentially run along the following lines:

Secret Commander: [to waiting neurons] Tell Conscious Mind to think 'tap finger'. And get that finger up.

A third of a second later …

Conscious Mind: I'll tap my finger … oh, hang on. Actually, I won't.

Finger: [remains still]

This is definitely an improvement on the conclusion that we are nothing more than automatons, deluded into thinking that we have some control over the course that our lives take. It also makes it OK once again to hold people morally responsible for their actions. According to this 'conscious veto' suggestion, there is nothing we can do to prevent the evil intentions that pop into our heads, but we do have the power to abort all plans to act on them. Phew. Restored back to the status of freely acting agents, we can relax … or can we? For consider this. What if the veto of the conscious mind over the orders of the secret commander came *itself* from the secret commander? According to this unflattering interpretation of what is going on behind the scenes – and it remains a disturbing possibility – the conscious mind is demoted right back to frilly accessory again:

Secret Commander: [to waiting neurons] Tell Conscious Mind to think 'tap finger'. And get that finger up.

Conscious Mind: I'll tap my finger …

Secret Commander: Change of plan. Somebody put the brakes on that finger. And don't forget to tell Conscious Mind to change its mind.

Conscious Mind: Oh, hang on. Actually, I won't tap my finger.

Finger: [remains still]

Creepy, or what? Fortunately, freedom of will – if indeed a conceit – is such a compelling one that it's easy enough to slip back into falling for the trick. Even philosophers, who have a tendency to dwell on these sorts of things, generally go happily about their everyday, if not their professional, lives without thinking twice about secret commanders and the rattling chains of foregone conclusions. There may well be a secret commander master-minding our every thought and deed, but at least he's discreet about it.

I hope that you've enjoyed this tour into the unconscious mind. Forget Freud, forget dreams, forget stretching out on a comfy leather sofa: cognitive psychology is the new spyhole into the psyche. (You may also wish to note that the cost of this entire book would barely buy you ten minutes of psychoanalysis.) Yet despite all of the astonishing discoveries that have been made about the unconscious in the last few decades, we should not lose our humility. Never forget that your unconscious is smarter than you, faster than you and more powerful than you. It may even control you. You will never know all of its secrets.

CHAPTER 7

The Weak-willed Brain

The prima donna within

My husband and I are finally in bed. Our toddler, who has been newly promoted from cot to bed, has been enjoying the ease with which he can now tumble out from under the covers, leave his bedroom and join us. It is an as yet unexplained mystery of the two-year-old brain why running down the hallway towards stony-faced parents is every bit as hilarious the thirtieth time as it is the first. The baby has been sleeping peaceably throughout this episode of bedtime rebellion – time that we should have been asleep ourselves. He was born fourteen weeks ago, and this is how long it has been since we last had an uninterrupted night's sleep. I am desperately, dangerously tired. My preoccupation with night-time awakenings consumes me to the point of obsession. Although I struggle to remember my own phone number, I can report with tedious precision the timing of each wail of the baby during the hours of darkness. I can calculate instantly the time lapsed between feedings – but forget words like 'spoon' and 'car'. I am exhausted. More than anything in the world, I crave sleep.

I cannot sleep.

I listen to the gentle, snuffling breathing of the baby. Extrapolating from the last few hellish nights, I estimate that I have perhaps 200 minutes in which to sleep before he wakes again. He stirs. I tense, waiting to see if he is waking up. He stays asleep. I now have approximately 199 minutes in which to sleep. Except, as I suddenly realise, it will take at least five minutes actually to drift off. One hundred and ninety-four minutes. So frustrating is it to be awake when I could be asleep that, perversely, I almost wish the baby would wake up.

One hundred and ninety-three minutes.

'Why don't you go to sleep?' mumbles my husband, roused by my fidgeting.

'I'm trying', I retort with all the patience I can muster, which is to say none. 'But I keep thinking about how little sleep I'm going to get before the baby needs feeding again.'

'That won't help', my husband advises. 'Think about something else.'

'I *can't*', I say. (I do not remember whether the 'you idiot' was spoken aloud or merely thought.)

My husband helpfully suggests a tip from an eight-week meditation course for which – in an uncharacteristic moment of spirituality I can only attribute to extreme sleep deprivation – he recently signed up.

'*Clear* your mind', he commands in the tongue-in-cheek New Age drawl he invariably assumes when conversation turns to the psychical realm. 'Don't think – *sense*. Focus on the *feeling* of the pillow against your cheek.' He sniggers, then goes back to sleep.

Obediently, I turn my attention to the feeling of the pillow against my cheek. But within a few seconds my mind decides that it has garnered all the interest there is to be had from this particular sensation. It is in too lively a mood, and quickly becomes bored. Instead, it focuses my unwilling, bleary eyes on the glowing clock-face. One hundred and ninety minutes and counting. Determined to get to sleep, I order my mind to return to soporific contemplation of the soft touch of the cotton-covered duck-feathers beneath my buzzing head. It ignores me. It has other matters to pursue: one hundred and eighty-nine minutes ... one hundred and eighty-eight ...

My mind has a mind of its own: I cannot even control my own thoughts. With all my might I exhort my will to rechannel the stream of consciousness but – although *I* am quite irredeemably wide awake – my will appears to be fast asleep.

It's hard work being in charge of a brain. Despite all the help it receives from the mental butler, the conscious self still finds its workload rather heavy. And, ironically, one of its more arduous duties involves keeping itself under control. Having decided to become a paragon of perfect living – to forgo desserts, stay late at work and stop thinking about that rather attractive next-door neighbour – it must then follow through. But, as Aristotle remarked (perhaps while reaching for his second slice of baklava), 'The hardest victory is the victory over self.' Willpower is set into battle against the impulse to indulge and – alas – it is all too often resolve that is the loser. You sharply order your mind to stop grinding on about that parking fine you got this morning, or your lack of sleep – but only sporadically does it deign to obey you. Self-control – as we all know to our chagrin – is a temperamental performer. Some mornings we are up with the birds and touching our toes a hundred times before leaping into a cold shower. At other times, the birds are taking their elevenses when we finally stop hitting the snooze button.

Some researchers have likened self-control, which strives, so often unsuccessfully, to keep us pure in thought and deed, to a 'moral muscle'.[1] This is because, like any muscle made of mere flesh and blood, it becomes fatigued with use. In fact, even quite modest feats of self-control leave you in a surprisingly weakened state so far as subsequent acts of self-restraint are concerned. Take, for example, a group of hungry volunteers who were left alone in a room containing both a tempting platter of freshly baked chocolate-chip cookies, and a plate piled high with radishes.[2] Some of the volunteers were asked to sample only the radishes. These peckish volunteers manfully resisted the temptation of the cookies and ate the prescribed number of radishes. (The effort of will this required was splendidly demonstrated by several partici-pants who were spotted, through a secret two-way mirror, picking up cookies and holding them up to their noses in order to inhale their aroma longingly.) Other, more fortunate, volunteers were asked to sample the cookies. In the next, supposedly unrelated, part of the experiment, the volunteers were asked to try to solve a difficult puzzle. The researchers weren't interested in whether the volunteers solved it. (In fact, it was unsolvable.) Rather, they wanted to know how long the volunteers would persist with it. Their self-control already depleted, volunteers forced to snack on radishes persisted for less than half as long as people who had eaten the cookies, or (in case you should think that chocolate cookies offer inner strength) other volunteers who had skipped the eating part of the experiment altogether.

In fact, it looks as if resisting temptation is only one of the many mentally taxing jobs done by the conscious self that drains the power of the moral muscle. Making decisions, getting things going, developing plans, fixing your attention on the task in hand – in short, anything that requires concentrated thought – all deplete the same pool of mental resources. This might explain why it's so hard to get anything done – even something as seemingly simple as switching off the television – after a hard day at work. With your inner battery dangerously low after a series of intellectually challenging situations throughout the workday, the will may be reluctant to do anything except put its feet up once you get home. In a simulation of the daily grind, some volunteers were given a highly mentally demanding task to do – the psychology lab equivalent of controlling air traffic.[3] The other volunteers were used more like factory workers: their job was so repetitive and easy that it quickly became automatic. Then the volunteers watched a video, which they could stop at any time by pressing down on a button. The film challenged even the very worst of television broadcasting. It was an unchanging shot of a blank white wall with a table and computer equipment in the foreground. Drained by their Herculean task in the first part of the experiment, the air traffic controllers found themselves slumped inertly in front of the TV screen for much longer than the factory workers, too sluggish to summon up the will to press a buzzer to end the show.

Nor is it just running the more business-like aspects of the self that saps resources. Keeping the more touchy-feely part of ourselves restrained is also tiring and, again, leaves us with less mental energy for other sorts of self-regulation. Some volunteers were asked to exercise self-restraint by keeping their faces as an inscrutable mask that concealed a turmoil of emotions. Afterwards, the researchers found, they had less strength of will left over with which to grapple with intellectually challenging tasks, compared with volunteers whose wills were fresh and unused.[4]

Indeed, putting on any sort of unfamiliar public face is an act that leaves your next performance, whatever it might be, a little lacking in oomph.[5] Volunteers recruited for an experiment were asked to bring along a friend who, they were told, would give them a mock interview. Some volunteers were told to respond to the questions in the modestly self-effacing manner that we normally assume with our friends (who know us well enough to be able to discern the light shining from under our bushels). Other volunteers, by contrast, were given the embarrassing job of shamelessly promoting themselves to their friend who, they knew, would have absolutely no idea why they had suddenly become such an obnoxious braggart.

Next, the interviewees were given a dauntingly long list of three-digit by three-digit multiplication problems to solve without the help of a calculator. The researchers instructed them to keep going until they'd completed all the problems, or decided to stop working. The self-lauding volunteers, who'd had to override the humility we normally portray while in the company of friends, had little nervous energy left to devote to computing the product of '234×889', and the like. Dropping their pencils in defeat a mere ten minutes into the exercise on average, they worked for about half as much time as did the other volunteers.

It's not just that talking the talk drains the resources available for you to walk the walk. As you might begin to fear, the unhappy consequences of a resource run dry also work the other way round: dipping into our limited mental means in order to complete a difficult job blights our chances of making a good impression. Cognitively drained, the uglier side of our nature begins to show through the cracks in the façade we usually present to others. In a series of experiments, researchers enfeebled volunteers with a variety of mentally demanding tasks, then sat back to observe the unfortunate effect this had on the volunteers' ability to present themselves in a good light.[6] Lacking the mental vigour necessary to keep their more objectionable tendencies in check, the mentally tired volunteers became either inappropriately loose-tongued, or coldly tight-lipped with strangers. And, sorry to say, they also made rather less effort than is customary to disguise the very good opinion they had of themselves.

The rapid burn-out suffered by the will is certainly a regrettable feature of our mental make-up. However, presumably we can be confident that the moral muscle, if well-rested, can be relied upon?

Unfortunately, it can't. The will is not only quickly tuckered out – it is also easily set off-kilter by a bad mood, and insists on cajoling itself back into good humour before it will return to its job of keeping you on the straight and narrow. Emotional distress shifts our priorities. We stop fixing our thoughts on how we want to look in our bathing suit this summer, the pink and healthy lungs we want to recover, or the down payment for the dream home we're saving for. Instead, we petulantly demand to be made to feel good again – *right now* – and impulsively reach for the comforting cookie, cigarette or luxury consumable.

To observe this change in focus from the long- to the short-term, researchers distressed some volunteers by asking them to imagine, as vividly as they could, how they would feel if they ran a red light, thereby causing an accident that killed a child.[7] Other volunteers had the happier task of imagining themselves saving a child's life. Then each person was ushered into a different room to take part in an 'unrelated taste test'. Bowls heaped temptingly high with goldfish crackers, chocolate-chip cookies and pretzels were placed before them. (The bowls were carefully weighed both before and after the unknowing volunteers were let loose on them.) In comparison to the more cheerful volunteers, people who, just before, had been deflated by the depressing exercise of the imagination gorged themselves – but only when they thought it would jolly them up. For in a twist on the familiar offering of food as comfort, some were informed before the taste test that, 'contrary to popular belief, scientific evidence shows that eating doesn't actually make you feel better'. The distressed volunteers who had been told this managed to stop themselves from over-indulging in the snack foods.

Likewise, in a similar sort of experiment, people who had been made miserable were advised to practise for an imminent maths test. They were then left to their own devices for quarter of an hour in a supposedly private room. Spied on through a slit in a curtained two-way mirror, these volunteers were observed reading trashy magazines, playing games and rifling nosily through desk drawers.[8] They spent barely more than a minute working on practice sums. But equally sad people told that their current low mood had been fixed to stay that way by an aroma-therapy candle showed much more resistance to the urge to pro-crastinate. Thinking that they were stuck with their gloomy feelings, they didn't attempt to cheer themselves up, but persisted with the sums. We *can* exert self-control when we're feeling blue – we just usually choose not to because it's more important to us to feel good than to be good.

Rested and content, then, the moral muscle is surely able and willing to perform its duties?

Well, no. Exquisitely sensitive to its audience, the will can also be put off its stride by rejection. Those of us who, as children, lacked sufficient physical or social coordination, will vividly remember from schooldays the tortuous process of 'picking teams' – the mounting dread that it will be you who, conspicuous in your rejection, will stand alone at the end, unwanted by either team. In a laboratory simulation of this childhood horror, researchers put people together into groups of half a dozen or so, and asked them to get to know one other.[9] Then each person was led to a private room, and asked to say which two of the other participants they would most like to work with for the next task. Some volunteers were randomly picked to be the popular kids: everyone wanted to work with them, they were told by the researchers. But because that wasn't possible (so the cover story continued) they would have to work alone. The other group of volunteers were made the rejects of the classroom. 'I hate to tell you this', fibbed the experimenter smoothly, 'but no one chose you as someone they wanted to work with. So I'll have you do the next task alone.' Each person was then left in private with a bowl of 35 chocolate-chip cookies to taste. He or she was told to eat as many as they needed to judge the taste, smell and texture. After a careful debriefing (which we will hope was adequate to combat the belief perseverance phenomenon we met in 'The Pig-headed Brain') the volunteer was thanked and dismissed.

The experimenter then counted up how many cookies were left in the bowl. Supposedly popular volunteers sampled about four cookies, on average. This, they clearly felt, was quite enough to offer a thoroughly researched opinion on their gastronomic qualities. By contrast (and in keeping with the stereotype of the social out-cast consoling himself with calories), the rejected volunteers felt the need to eat twice as many cookies to do the same job.

Perhaps, you may think, they were simply buoying up their spirits after the unpleasantness of the first part of the experiment. But it seemed not. Further studies showed it was something else entirely that put self-control on strike. Using a new technique for making people feel bad, the researchers gave a fresh set of students bogus feedback on a personality questionnaire. Some were told that their scores revealed that they were the sort of person who would end up rejected, miserable and lonely later in life. 'You may have friends and relationships now', they were warned, 'but by your mid-twenties most of these will have drifted away. You may even marry or have several marriages, but these are likely to be short-lived and not continue into your thirties.' (Indeed, the experimenter all but guaranteed that their corpse would lie rotting in a bedsit for weeks after their death until finally discovered by the gas man.) Other volunteers were led to expect a different type of misfortune: that they would be highly accident-prone later in life. Their limbs would crack like twigs underfoot, cars would accidentally mow them down. Later life, in short, would be nothing short of a gruesome slapstick.

Having sealed each volunteer's fate in this way, the experimenter ushered them to the next phase of the experiment. Fitting a pair of headphones snugly about their ears, the experimenter explained that each ear would hear something different. Rather than enjoy the interesting speech on a policy issue that flowed into their right ear, they must attend only to the dull stream of random words trickling into their left. So that the experimenter could see how well the volunteers were able to control their attention, they were asked to write down every word spoken into their left ear that contained the letter 'm' or 'p'. People who had been forecast a life of wretched aloneness achieved only a very desultory score on this task. Their attention disobediently straying, they missed nearly a quarter of the words that they should have jotted down. The other volunteers, by contrast, managed a much more enthusiastic performance, with a 90 per cent success rate.

The researchers, wondering why the prospect of social exclusion (but not a different type of misfortune) should make people less able or willing to control the direction of their attention, checked whether it was a particularly sad mood in the 'future loneliness' volunteers that was disrupting their strength of will. However, the results of mood-rating questionnaires (which all the volunteers filled out before putting on their headphones) showed that people threatened with a future of loneliness were no lower in spirits than were the other volunteers. Poor mood, then, could not have been the reason why telling people that they would live unloved made them so careless at the listening task.[10]

Perhaps, the researchers wondered, being told that you are essentially unlikable makes you loath to direct your attention inwards, for fear of the personal deficiencies and flaws – the very reasons for your rejection by others – that you may unearth. Remaining steadfastly determined not to think about yourself certainly helps to keep you safe from disturbing self-revelations. But at the same time, ignoring the inner self leaves you unable to make the usual sorts of comparisons between 'what I am doing' and 'what I *should* be doing' that are so essential for keeping the self in line. If this was the problem with people made to feel unlikable, the researchers reasoned, then forcing the rejected volunteers' attention back upon themselves should bring their self-regulation back into action. They achieved this by using a surprisingly commonplace piece of equipment – a mirror. Lo and behold, this humble household item was all that was needed to reverse completely the damaging effects of social exclusion. Some 'future loneliness' volunteers were casually placed in front of a mirror for the listening task and, confronted with their reflections, were compelled to self-reflect. As a result, they listened every bit as proficiently to the string of random words as did the other volunteers whose egos had been left intact.

The will, we are learning, has a list of dressing-room demands as long as that of the most egotistical celebrity. It must not be over-worked. It must have only happiness and light around it. And, as we have just discovered, it must feel beloved and cherished at all times. What is more, although under trying and difficult circumstances it may valiantly cry that 'the show must go on!', the will's attempts to rise above adversity are often rather unsuccessful. Stress and distraction both have very untoward effects on the conscious mind's ability to stay focused and in control of itself. It's strange but true that, the harder we try to relax and forget our anxieties, the more determined we are to cheer up and forget our troubles, or the more urgently we try to wind down and sleep, the more persistently thoughts of stress, sadness or sleeplessness can drum at consciousness.

Why is it that our thoughts can be so unruly? It is not often that I have cause to note deficiencies common to both the observations offered up by my husband and the writings of the great philosopher René Descartes. But had the famous thinker been with us that night I lay tossing and turning in bed, unable to sleep, he might well have added to my husband's advice an admonition from his own philosophy that, if there is anything in this world that we can and should conquer, it is our own thoughts.[11] But, as all but the most accomplished at meditation would agree, a nagging thought is an extremely tough adversary.

The problem arises from the way that the brain goes about mental control. According to ironic process theory, both you (the conscious you, that is) and your unconscious mental processes work together to keep unwanted thoughts out of mind.[12] When this collaboration is rolling along the way it should, you successfully manage to direct your attention away from the sorts of thoughts you are trying to avoid. Rather than becoming lost in the worrying thoughts that sometimes like to crowd in at bedtime, instead you peacefully concentrate on counting a stupefying number of sheep, or on the pleasant cushioning of your face by your pillow. Meanwhile, down below, the mental butler is busy scanning any mental packages that could be on their way up the stairs to consciousness. It knows that you're easily sidetracked so it is on the lookout for any traces of alertness that might undo your attempts to stay sleepy. When it finds a suspect looking package, it immediately alerts the authorities. 'Watch out', it hisses up the stairway. 'You're starting to think about your tax return.' You quickly renew efforts to distract yourself from unwelcome thoughts, and peace reigns once again.

Unfortunately, as the mental butler rummages through your mental baggage searching for illegal stowaways, it actually primes the very sorts of thoughts it is looking for. It disturbs them, bringing them to the verge of wakefulness. This, as you know from the previous chapter, ironically makes those thoughts *more* likely to reach consciousness. When the conscious self is on top form, with no other business to deal with, this is easily dealt with. You respond so quickly to the mental butler's warnings that your attention barely wavers from its desired target.

But, as we know, the conscious is not very good at multi-tasking. If, at the same time, you are also trying to deal with the sorts of irritations that so often plague us – the blare of next door's television, the stresses of work or family, the needling awareness of the countdown of the clock – then you are in trouble. Unable to do two things properly, you fail to respond to the mental butler's cautions that unwanted thoughts are about to burst forth into consciousness. Suddenly, you find that you are thinking about your tax return, and here comes the ironic part of ironic process theory. Because the mental butler has been thumping about, priming those very sorts of thoughts you want to avoid, when your conscious defences are down these unwelcome intrusions are actually *more* likely to rush in than if you had never set yourself the goal of keeping them at bay. By trying to control our thoughts, we actually plant the very seeds of our own undoing, as the author of the theory, Daniel Wegner, puts it. When the burden on the conscious self is too great, it is our very attempts to keep certain sorts of thoughts out of mind that make them hurtle in – and in far greater numbers than if we had not attempted to follow Descartes' stricture to conquer our thoughts.

For example, in an experiment close to my heart, Wegner and his colleagues showed how our minds can unwittingly act against us as we struggle to get to sleep.[13] Volunteers were given a Walkman to wear to bed, told to press 'play' once they had tucked themselves in for the night, and asked to follow whatever instructions they heard. The voice on the tape told some of them simply to go to sleep whenever they felt like it. Other volunteers, by contrast, were told that the job of falling asleep was an urgent and pressing one. They should fall asleep as quickly as they possibly could. They all then drifted off to the soothing sounds of bubbling streams and gentle bird-song that followed the instructions on the tape. People told to fall asleep quickly did, indeed, reach the land of Nod sooner than those left to fall asleep in their own time. Feeling calm and untrammelled thanks to the relaxing sounds of nature, the conscious self was able to put its full strength to the task. With perfect teamwork, mental downstairs and upstairs together ensured that only restful thoughts reached consciousness, and slumber soon followed.

Two other groups of volunteers were not so lucky with the music allocated to them by the experimenter, however. Instead of sleep-conducive New Age sounds, they (poor lambs) had to listen to the rousing marching band music of John Philip Sousa. Again, some volunteers were left to fall asleep in their own time, while others were ordered to go to sleep as quickly as they could. But this time, it was those left to their own devices who first found themselves nestling in the arms of Morpheus. Time-pressured volunteers, setting the process of mental control into action in order to get themselves to sleep quickly, became paradoxically wakeful. Driven to distraction by the stirring sounds of Sousa, the mental upstairs could not cope at the same time with its role of keeping thoughts in check. As a result, floodgates were opened to the wakeful thoughts primed by the mental butler. It actually took them *longer* to get to sleep, compared to those who were making no special efforts to do so quickly.

There are, it seems, so many reasons for will to fail us that it is a wonder we ever manage to keep our thoughts and impulses in rein. The will is feeble, drained by emotions; it is thin-skinned, and has woefully limited powers of concentration.

But let us look on the bright side – at least there is plenty of room for improvement. These insights into when and why our will is *not* done offer, if not solutions, then some pointers, at least, as to how to keep willpower healthy and strong. What, for example, can best be done about this unfortunate tendency of the moral muscle to become fatigued with use? One option, of course, is to use it only very sparingly. My father, a professional philosopher, has a job that involves thinking very hard about very difficult things. This, of course, is an activity that consumes mental resources at a terrific rate. The secret of his success as an academic, I am now convinced, is to ensure that none of his precious brainpower is wasted on other, less important matters. He feels the urge to sample a delicious luxury chocolate? He pops one in his mouth. Pulling on yesterday's shirt less trouble than finding a clean one? Over his head the stale garment goes. Rather fancies sitting in a comfy armchair instead of taking a brisk jog around the park? Comfy armchair it is. Thanks to its five-star treatment, my father's willpower – rested and restored whenever possible – can take on the search for wisdom with the strength of ten men.

Although we may not all be able to live the charmed life of the well-paid scholar, the general principle – not to spread our inner resolve too thin – is an important one. If your New Year's Resolutions list reads:

1. Give up smoking

2. Begin punishing new exercise regime

3. Eat only cabbage soup for breakfast, lunch and dinner

then you will almost certainly fail. There is simply not enough willpower to go around. Pick the most important fight, and concentrate on that.

Interestingly, this seems to be what we do naturally when confronted with a grim reminder of our mortality. Researchers asked one group of students to recollect the September 11 tragedy (where they were when they heard the news, their thoughts and feelings).[14] Other people were asked the same questions about a fire on campus that had happened at about the same time, one which, fortunately, had claimed no lives. They were then offered a choice of fruit salad or chocolate cake, supposedly as thanks for taking part in the experiment. The morbid thoughts triggered by thinking about the deaths on September 11 focused the minds of the students very sharply on what was important to them. People whose esteem was heavily invested in their physical appearance were much more likely to select the fruit salad, compared with equally vain people whose thoughts had recently dwelled on the campus fire. (So, if you are such a person, keeping a skull in the fridge could be just the ticket for keeping fingers from straying towards calorie-loaded temptations.) The attitude of other people, though – people who regarded their bodies more as hotels for their brains than ends in themselves – was to eat, drink and be merry. These volunteers were more, not less, likely to tuck-in to the chocolate cake if they had just been reminded that tomorrow they might die.

A third strategy for keeping the moral muscle bolstered for when we need it most is to offer it regular exercise. Although exercising self-restraint wears out the will in the short term, it seems that over time, like its physical counterparts, the moral muscle becomes taut and bulging from use. Researchers asked people to exert self-control by not thinking about a white bear for five minutes.[15] (If you try this yourself you will discover that this is quite a tricky thing to do.[16]) So the researchers could see how much this mental exercise tired willpower, both before and afterwards, they asked volunteers to squeeze together a hand-grip for as long as they possibly could. This task also required self-control, to overcome the urge to relax. Sapped by the intervening act of not thinking about white bears, unsurprisingly, the volunteers released the hand-grip more quickly the second time round.

What the researchers wanted to know, though, was whether they could build up the strength of people's moral muscle by exercising it. With this aim in mind, they asked some of the volunteers to practise self-restraint over the coming few weeks: by monitoring and improving their posture, for example.[17] For two weeks, they were told, they should resist their natural tendency to sit slumped like a sack of potatoes and amble sway-backed from here to there. Instead they were to stay strictly erect at all times, and deport themselves as though a book were balanced atop their head. Other volunteers, by way of contrast, were left to live their own sweet way for the fortnight. When the two weeks were up, all the volunteers returned to the lab. Once more, they were put through their paces: squeezing the hand-grip, suppressing thoughts of white bears, then back to the hand-grip again. For people whose wills had been lounging idly for two weeks, the thought-control exercise left the moral muscle as flaccidly exhausted as before. Drooping from its labours after the thought-control exercise, their moral muscle again gave in to the spring of the hand-grip much more easily than before. But the willpower of the other group, perky and toned by the fortnight of training, was now left almost untouched by its wrestles with white bears. Thanks to this newfound endurance, their final session with the hand-grip showed that they were now much better able to withstand the debilitating effects of their earlier self-restraint.

Moving on now to the will's exquisite sensitivity to the prevailing emotional and social climate, is there anything that can be done to keep the will working even when you are feeling sad and unloved? Perhaps the best we can do in these circumstances is to remember that the problem is not that we can no longer control ourselves, but that we are simply less inclined to do so. Remember that low-spirited people who were told that giving in to temptation would not improve their mood restrained themselves from eating chocolate-chip cookies just as well as did people in a more positive frame of mind. (Funnily enough – in a rare occurrence indeed for a social psychology experiment – there may have been an element of truth to the claim made by the experimenter that eating wouldn't make them feel better. Although there was no doubt a momentary pleasure to be had from scoffing cookies, it seemed to be gone no sooner than had the last crumb been wiped from the chin. When the experimenter asked the participants about their mood – right after the supposed 'taste test' – there was no sign that cookies, once down the gullet, continued to bring happiness. It may be in vain that we attempt to assuage ill-humour by spoiling ourselves.)

The loss of will that comes from rejection from a cruel world can, like the enervating effect of feeling blue, also be overcome.

What seems to be the key here is resisting the natural tendency to avoid potentially bruising self-reflection. Those who have just snubbed you may be somewhat startled when you immediately whip out from your pocket a mirror, into which you begin to intently gaze, but – who knows – it could be worth a try.

However carefully the will is nurtured and ministered to, though, a problem remains, as we have discovered. It is hard to be single-minded as we go about our pursuits. The mind easily falls prey to mental distractions, having only poor powers of concentration. As the ironic process theory points out, when the mind wavers from its intended project of keeping certain sorts of musings out of mind, perversely, we find ourselves besieged with those very thoughts we most wish to avoid. Keeping life simple, calm, and sensibly paced may be a necessity, rather than an indulgence, if we are to keep our thoughts under control, suggests Daniel Wegner.[18] And when our lives are a far, far cry from the Zen-like tranquillity that would be most ideal, we may be better off giving up altogether on the doomed mission, and allowing our thoughts to flow freely. Better a trickle of unpleasant thoughts to deal with than a torrent. This, I now know, was my great mistake on that sleepless night. With too many other things already on my mind, which is so often the case for people with insomnia, I was fighting a losing battle with my recalcitrant will. Curiously, what I should have done was try my utmost to stay awake. Insomniacs ordered at bedtime to stop themselves from falling asleep actually get to sleep more quickly than usual. The reason, according to ironic process theory, is that the sleep-starved person calls off her inevitably unsuccessful attempts to keep wakeful thoughts suppressed. With the mental butler no longer priming those very thoughts, they are much less likely to end up bursting into consciousness to keep her awake.[19]

Take all of these lessons to heart, by all means. But there is even better stuff to come. If we have learned anything so far in this chapter, it is that the will is capricious and temperamental – it is the prima donna within. Stood beside the no-fuss mental butler – which is tireless, efficient and superbly capable – one might be justified in drawing rather unfavourable comparisons. Wouldn't it be wonderful if you could bypass that sketchy, off-on willpower altogether? Imagine if, like an idle but cunning dictator, you could exploit the vast power of the unconscious to serve your own ends …

Well, you can! But it does take some work on your part. Remember from the previous chapter that goals, acted on over and over in particular situations, come to be automatically set off by cues in the environment. For example, without even realising it, people who thought it was important to make mother proud worked harder on a word task after thinking about mum. This helpful characteristic of the mental butler can be exploited to your great advantage when it comes to ensuring that noble and worthy goals triumph over base and shameful impulses. If you are disciplined about resisting a particular sort of temptation whenever it appears seductively on the horizon, then sooner or later your unconscious will reward you by joining the tussle on your behalf. The tempting situation itself automatically sets off the goal to resist.

This helpful trick can even have you turning up your nose at chocolate, as the happy findings of some extraordinary research have shown.[20] Researchers found themselves a group of women students who were all at least a little 'ooh, I shouldn't eat that' about food. One at a time, each woman was taken into a small office strewn with magazines and other props carefully chosen to set the woman's unconscious working in a particular way. In the 'diet prime' office, the surfaces were covered with magazines about exercise and dieting, with flyers for weight-watching classes pinned to the walls. Other women were led into the 'temptation prime' office. Here, the magazine of choice was Chocolatier, with various chocolate-based food items left lying around the office for good measure. For a third group of women, who were being used as a boring comparison group, the magazines were about economics or geography. The volunteer sat in the artfully decorated office while she did a computer task that revealed the clandestine effect of the priming on her unconscious. She saw a series of letter strings and in each case had to decide, as quickly as possible, whether it was a proper word (and included among these was the word 'diet'), or a nonsense word. Then – oh so casually – she was asked to select either a Twix bar or an apple, as thanks for her participation in the experiment.

As you might expect from what we learned in the previous chapter, women in the diet prime office were quicker to recognise the word 'diet' than were women in the comparison group. The diet schema activated, words from this schema leapt into consciousness in the word-recognition task. What is more, the goals of the diet schema also activated, nearly two-thirds of these women chose an apple instead of a Twix. This showed impressive restraint over the norm, since nearly two-thirds of the women from the comparison group (who saw the economics and geography magazines) chose the Twix. The unobtrusive priming of the diet schema successfully tempered the women's natural tendency to choose the chocolate.

You may, at this point, begin to fear for the women in the temptation prime condition. Did they, you may wonder, not only grab the Twix, but then raid the experimenter's office for the rest of his supplies? In fact, no. Because these women were used to gastronomic self-denial, the unconscious had set up a strong and automatic link between the temptation schema and the diet schema – the tempting images themselves primed the diet schema. As a result, these women were not only just as quick to recognise the word 'diet' as were the women in the diet prime condition – they also showed an equal abstemiousness. The fleeting allure of short-term gratification was successfully and immediately squelched: hurrah!

This is all very cheering, but there is still the drawback that we have to put in a bit of legwork ourselves first. The unconscious only starts pulling its weight once you have a solid history of resisting temptation through conscious effort behind you. If you are the sort of person who responds, 'ooh, *lovely*' when offered a slice of cake, your unconscious will make few efforts to activate the schema of self-restraint in the face of temptation.[21] You can't go around throwing sweeties down your gullet and expect the unconscious to get the right idea. Boring though it is, you need to develop good habits for this willpower-enhancing strategy to work.

Fortunately though, psychologists seem to have discovered a way in which we can develop good habits, instantly. The secret is not just to make a resolution. ('I will write a book before my baby is born.') You must also work out exactly how and when you will do it. (Of course if your partner, like mine, draws a salary from bossing people about, this bit may be worked out for you.) To use the grandly official jargon, you must form an 'implementation intention'.[22] ('I will sit at my desk immediately after breakfast every weekend, and every day of my annual leave, and write so many words a day until it is done.')

These implementation intentions can have near-magical effects on us, it appears. People who beef up their resolves with a simple but determined plan of action are far more likely to become one of those irritating types who shame the rest of us as they virtuously jog past in an ostentatious display of self-discipline. Students panicked by vivid descriptions of the slow but sure narrowing of arteries in people whose hearts enjoy an uninterruptedly leisurely pace of life, fully intended to take some vigorous exercise at least once in the week that followed.[23] But the road to coronary heart disease is paved with good intentions: two-thirds of the students found that they had 'forgotten', 'been too busy' or 'just didn't get round to it' by the end of the week. In fact, they didn't exercise any more that week than students who hadn't been shown the health education leaflet about coronary heart disease.

Another group of students, though – given the same terrifying leaflet about the damaging effects of a sedentary lifestyle – were also made to plan exactly when, where and how they would get their hearts thumping from physical exertion. And they were true to their word. In stark contrast to the dismal efforts of the other students, a remarkable 91 per cent of them remembered to exercise, found time for it and did actually get round to doing it. Likewise, implementation intentions also improve, to a striking extent, the chances that we will reach for an apple in lieu of a chocolate bar, recycle paper cups, finish work on time, or take the trouble to examine vulnerable portions of our anatomy for signs of disease.[24] (Sadly, though, the seemingly miraculous powers of implementation intentions are apparently inadequate to overcome the inertia that sets in at the dismal prospect of flossing our teeth.)[25]

How do implementation intentions work their wonders upon us? By handing over control to the faithful unconscious. When we confidently and sincerely proclaim that, 'When I visit the canteen at lunchtime I will buy an apple instead of a Twix', the mental butler alerts the unconscious of your plans, and it adjusts itself accordingly. The part of your brain that represents the canteen is put on high alert. Then, like the habitual and successful dieter whose unconscious has built up a strong link between fatloaded treats and the aim of resisting their appeal, the intention of buying an apple is automatically set off the instant you walk into the canteen. With a single act of will (which, frankly, seems to be about as much as we can expect from this undependable part of ourselves), the conscious self can take a much-needed rest and leave the remainder of the job to the more reliable unconscious brain.

'Where there's a will, there's a way', it is said. But what if the will is unwilling? The will is a highly temperamental performer. Cast it in too many performances and it will collapse onstage halfway through the act. Upset or insult it, and it will lock itself in the dressing room and refuse to come out. Distract it, worry it or put it under pressure and it will hit bum notes. The prima donna of the brain, the will must be handled with the utmost care. Only if its many needs are ministered to is there a chance that – just sometimes – it will gift us the strength to pursue the thoughts and deeds we intend.

But with only 188 minutes of uninterrupted sleep to be had at night? Not a chance.

CHAPTER 8

The Bigoted Brain

'Thug ... tart ... slob ... nerd ... airhead'

My husband's first experience of Scotland was a formative one, from which I fear he has never fully recovered. We travelled across the border to Berwick for a wedding, and booked into a not inexpensive bed and breakfast. Now the Scots do have a certain reputation for, shall we say, a propensity towards thrift. We were, however, prepared to assume that the absence of any soap in our room was an oversight – until, that is, we were sharply informed, in response to our inquiry, that the provision of soap was deemed to be the responsibility of the guest. My husband was somewhat taken aback by this. In his native New Zealand, any B & B guest considers himself much neglected if large quantities of hand-crafted Manuka honey soap are not lavished upon him. 'So it's true, what they say about Scots', he remarked with glee, delighted to have been treated so soon to an apparent vindication of the stereotype.

But there was a far more challenging horror to greet us in the morning. We sat down to breakfast, tired and hungover after the wedding, and waited impatiently for the pot of tea to brew. Every few minutes my husband would dribble another splash of pale gold water into his cup, then return the pot to the table with an angry clatter. After about ten minutes of this, he decided that further investigation was required. He lifted the teapot lid and peered inside. His eyes, when they rose to meet mine, were wide with disbelief. In awe, he whispered to me, 'There are no tea bags in there. Not *one*!'

He was quiet and thoughtful on the long drive home. Every so often he would break the silence to ask, 'Do you suppose they use the *same* tea bag to make everyone's pot of tea?' or to speculate, 'Perhaps each table has its own dedicated bag, which is pegged up to dry on a little line, ready for the next morning.'

Possibly, given this experience, I should have been more understanding of my husband's response to my telling him about our bigoted brains. Over dinner, I explained how it is that pernicious stereotypes colour our every interpretation of others' behaviour, and even have the power to generate self-fulfilling prophecies of our stereotypical beliefs. With eloquent passion, I told him of our ignoble habit of using stereotypes to boost our egos, and the subtle but devastating effects of stereotypes on stereotyped groups. Finally, my dinner cold and untouched on my plate in noble sacrifice to his edification, I described the devious tricks the brain uses to discount evidence that contradicts our stereotypical beliefs, thus condemning us all to an eternally prejudiced and damaging perspective of our fellow humans.

'Ye-es', said my husband hesitantly, when I had finally stopped talking. 'But the Scots really *are* mean.'

As I said, given the trauma of a post-wedding breakfast without a nice strong cup of tea, I should have been more understanding. But I wasn't.

'*That*', I retorted angrily, 'is just the sort of thing an affluent white male *would* say.'

However egalitarian you may be (or think you are), your brain is stuffed with stereotypes. You may not personally subscribe to the view that women are nurturing, that black men are aggressive, or that Jews keep a tight grip on their wallets, but you can't pretend not to know that these are stereotypical traits of women, blacks and Jews. Stereotypes are a subgroup of the schemas that we met in 'The Secretive Brain', the filing system the brain uses to organise information into various categories. Like all schemas, in people schemas (or stereotypes), all the information about a certain group – homosexuals, the unemployed, Asians – is closely inter-twined in the brain. This means that if you use one bit of the schema – even just to be able to say 'Ah, an Asian' – then all the other parts of the Asian schema get restless. As a result, information in the Asian stereotype is more likely to be used by the brain, as it goes about the difficult job of interpreting the complicated and often ambiguous behaviour of those around us.

In a classic demonstration of this, some volunteers were sub-liminally primed with flashes of words (mostly negative) related to the black stereotype.[1] These included words such as 'lazy', 'welfare', 'unemployed', 'ghetto' and 'basketball'. Now one of the most commonly reported traits of the black stereotype is aggres-siveness, but the researcher was careful not to include any words related to aggression in the priming. She reasoned that, it being an intimate bedfellow of the other parts of the black stereotype, it would get awakened by the stirrings anyway. That this indeed happened – and its effect on the volunteers' decoding of another person's behaviour – was revealed by the second part of the experiment. The volunteers were asked to give their impressions of a character called Donald. Donald did things that could be viewed as either hostile or assertive, such as refusing to pay his rent until his flat was repainted. People whose black stereotype had been primed judged Donald to be significantly more hostile than did other volunteers not primed in the same way. The volunteers weren't aware that the stereotype had been activated (they hadn't even been aware of the flashed words) but it still had the power to colour their judgment of Donald.

The disturbing implication is that when dealing with a black man, the black stereotype is primed and ready to distort our interpretation of his every word and deed.[2] We might, for example, mistake the wallet he is pulling from his pocket for a gun. In 1999, four white New York police officers were acquitted of shooting an unarmed black man on the grounds that they had made this very mistake and thought that their lives were in danger. The officers may well have been speaking the truth, but would their eyes have deceived them in the same way had their unfortunate victim, Amidou Diallo, been white? Quite possibly not, suggests research using stereotype priming. Student volunteers were shown pairs of images: a face, followed by either a handgun or a hand tool.[3] They were told to ignore the face, which flashed up briefly supposedly to signal that the next image was about to appear, and to then identify the second picture as a gun or tool as quickly as possible by pressing one or other of two keys. Half of the time the face was black; the rest of the time it was white. The volunteers were much quicker at identifying the handguns when they were preceded by a black face, showing that perception itself was influenced by the racial priming. More disturbing still, however, was the discovery that volunteers, when under heavy pressure to classify the object quickly (as a police officer would often be), were more likely to mistake tools for handguns when they had just seen a black face. This suggests that the New York officers might have held their fire for a few extra, potentially life-saving milliseconds had Amidou Diallo been white.

Indeed, any suspicions we have that ethnicity might have played a part in this fatal shooting of an unarmed man by police (and other sad incidents like it) are all but confirmed by subsequent research. In a similar sort of experiment deliberately reminiscent of the killing of Marquise Hudspeth (who was shot by police officers who mistook his cellular phone for a weapon), non-black volunteers were shown a succession of pictures of different men, who were either black or white.[4] Each man appeared against an innocuous background, holding either a gun or a non-lethal item such as a wallet or phone. In each case, the volunteers had to decide whether to shoot (if the man was armed) or hold fire (if the man were merely about to make a phone call, say). The appearance of a white face together with a gun had an inappropriately soothing effect on the would-be police officers: they were far more likely to mistakenly hold their fire than if it was a black man wielding a weapon. And the inequity did not end there, of course: innocently unarmed black men were in far more danger of being shot at than were unarmed white men. Indeed, so pernicious is the stereotype of the dangerous black man that it

influenced black participants in just the same way: they showed
just the same racial bias in the experiment.

Nor can we cling to the comforting, if improbable, hope that
real law enforcement officers – painstakingly trained in racial
sensitivities and ethnic sensibilities – might show a reassuring
even-handedness in their propensity to shoot innocent passers-
by on the street. A similar sort of 'Shoot' or 'Hold Fire' experiment that recruited police officers from Florida as its participants
revealed that – when it comes to black men – they, like the rest of
us, tend to shoot first and ask questions later.[5] This is worrisome
indeed, particularly when officers are encouraged to take a trigger-
happy approach to policing – as in London following the bomb
attacks in July 2005 when Jean Charles de Menezes, a Brazilian,
was wrongly identified as a suicide bomber and shot dead. Bearing
the results of this research in mind, Londoners of ethnic origin
may want to think twice before running to catch a bus.

It's easy to see from these experiments, and the many others
like them, how viewing other people through bigot goggles helps
to reinforce stereotyped beliefs. We see what we expect to see. But
does it make a difference whether or not we subscribe to those
beliefs in the first place? Does the genuinely open-minded liberal
see others through bigot goggles just the same, or does she rise
loftily above such distortions? The answer seems to depend on
how the stereotype is primed. For example, a British study
primed the black stereotype by using only neutral words (like
'Brixton', 'dreadlocks' and 'reggae'). For non-racists, this had no
damaging effects on their impressions of other people's behaviour.[6] However, even this neutral priming influenced the racists

– they judged that the person they were evaluating suffered from the stereotypical faults of black people: unreliability and aggressiveness. What this suggests is that only in racists will seeing a black person automatically trigger the full-blown negative stereotype.

This is good news, but there is an important proviso. If what is primed is the *negative* stereotype, then even the non-prejudiced are susceptible to seeing the world through the biasing lens of that stereotype. In the same British study, when pejorative priming words were used (such as 'unemployed', 'dirty' or 'crime'), even the non-racists formed a more disapproving impression of the person they had to evaluate. What this means with regard to the real world is that no-holds-barred stereotyped portrayals of people will unconsciously affect the judgments of *everyone*, not just the bigot.

What, in that case, is the effect on the decent modern man of that device most beloved of advertisers everywhere: the sexy woman (or erotic part thereof)? To find out, two groups of men were shown a tape of television adverts.[7] One group of men watched mostly sexist adverts in which women were portrayed as sex objects. The other men watched ads without any sexual imagery. Next, each volunteer was asked to do a supposedly unrelated experiment: deciding whether or not a string of letters flashed on a computer screen was a word. Men who had watched the sexist adverts, unlike the other men, were quicker to recognise sexist words like 'babe' and 'bimbo' than less offensive words like 'mother' and 'sister'. This showed that the ads had done their job of priming the schema of women as sexual objects.

It was then time to see how this affected the men when they had to interact with a real, live woman. The men were asked, as a favour to the experimenter, to interview a female job candidate. The influence of the sexist ads on the dynamics of this interview was extraordinary. The men who had just watched women portrayed as sex-things – even the non-sexist men – sat closer to the interviewee, flirted more and asked her a greater number of sexually inappropriate questions, compared with the other men. The sexist adverts also biased the men's memory of the candidate, and their ability to gauge her qualifications. The sex-primed men remembered a great deal about the woman's physical appearance, but far less information that would help them to decide her suitability for the job. This didn't stop them from rating her as less competent, however. Despite this, these men were still more likely than the other group to recommend hiring the woman, perhaps because they found her more friendly and attractive than did the non-primed men. A meagre comfort, indeed, for women seeking gainful employment – especially when you consider that all of these shameful changes in the men came from them watching a few sex-pots draped over cars or around beer bottles.

This experiment doesn't just demonstrate that you should never, ever tell a woman who complains about sexist adverts to lighten up. It also highlights the second dangerous power of stereotypes: their capacity to change our *own* behaviour. In fact, you already saw this phenomenon in action in 'The Secretive Brain'. Remember, for example, the volunteers who ambled at a snail's pace down the hallway after having their elderly schema primed? Benign as this may sound, the trouble begins when you add another person into the social equation. Your behaviour has a knock-on effect on *their* behaviour and suddenly, without anyone having an inkling about it, you have all the ingredients of a self-fulfilling prophecy. Seeing a black person triggers the stereotype of the aggressive, hostile black. You, acting in line with the stereotype, behave aggressively yourself, which in turn leads the maligned person to respond in kind. You notice his hostility and, not realising your own role in their behaviour, the stereotype is confirmed in your mind.

Social psychologists have witnessed vicious circles of just this sort. For example, white people subliminally primed with black faces respond in a more hostile way to a request by the experimenter to redo a tedious computer task, compared with people primed with white faces.[8] The researchers wondered whether this primed aggressiveness might, in turn, make anyone on the receiving end of it more antagonistic in return.[9] One group of volunteers had the black stereotype subliminally primed using faces of black men, whereas the control group volunteers were primed with white faces. Then the volunteers were asked to play a quiz game with another (white) person. (The volunteers' quiz partners had to be white because a black partner would also prime the black stereotype in the control group, and might arouse suspicions regarding the nature of the experiment.) Just as the researchers predicted, the black-primed volunteers behaved more aggressively than volunteers primed with white faces. But what's more, this affected their quiz partner, who responded by getting bolshy right back. This didn't go unnoticed by the volunteers, who rated their partners as more hostile than did the control group volunteers.

What is most creepy about self-fulfilling stereotypes is that when you project your stereotypical beliefs onto someone, the image that gets bounced back is more a reflection of your own behaviour than of his or her true qualities. Yet your role in this horrible distortion goes undetected. The most well-meaning intention to be impartial when evaluating job applicants, for example, may be thoroughly undermined by your own behaviour. When white people were asked to interview a job applicant, they behaved very differently depending on whether the applicant was black or white.[10] This was despite the fact that the applicants were actually stooges, carefully trained to perform in a standard manner during the interview. If the applicant was black, the interviewers kept themselves more physically distant, made more speech errors during the interview and ended it more abruptly.

A dispiriting follow-up study showed that being treated like a black person in this way could undermine anyone's interview performance. White Princeton University students were interviewed for a job by trained stooges. Half were given the remote, inarticulate and terse style of interview that black applicants received in the first experiment. This 'black treatment' hampered the white Princeton students: judges watching the interviews rated them as significantly less competent for the job than students given the 'white treatment'. This experiment shows that relatively subtle differences in the way that white people respond to black people compared to white people may undermine black job applicants' true abilities, making them seem less competent than they really are. Then, not only does that black person not get the job, but the impression that black people tend not to be quite up to scratch becomes engrained a little more strongly in the interviewer's mind.

Even when a person from a disparaged group – despite the unfair odds set up by stereotyping – manages to clinch a job, the battle may have only just begun. The gates to traditionally masculine domains may have been grudgingly cracked open to women, for example, but it seems that men are still rather jittery about the ability of the 'weaker sex' to cope. Men and women volunteers were set up as the team leaders of a group of male and female subordinates.[11] The task at hand was a portfolio of particularly traditionally 'male' maths and reasoning problems (war games and sports problems, for example). As the boss, the team leader's responsibility was to choose who would, or would not, join the team, and to fill the various hierarchical positions in whatever way would enable them to best compete against other teams. Doing well on the task, they were told, would bring substantial monetary rewards. And, as in life, the bonuses received by their various team members would be commensurate with the seniority of their position in the team. The only information the team leader had to go on in the selection process was the input his or her underlings provided about their academic strengths or weaknesses and, seemingly incidentally, their gender. In fact, the information offered by the minions, who were supposedly in another room, was carefully made up by the experimenter and delivered to the unsuspecting team leader by email.

The women team leaders, considering their pool of candidates for ways in which weaknesses in team members might drag down the team, recognised that there was no good reason to think that the men would perform any better than the women.

They were completely even-handed in the way that they allocated team positions (and thus earning potential) to their fictional subordinates. But the men were clearly concerned that the stereotypical woolly and irrational 'feminine' qualities of the women might hamper their team's chances for success. They showed blatant sex discrimination, with men disproportionately represented in the better spots in the team. But by way of compensation for the side-lined women, they lavished them with disingenuous compliments: 'Your answers were excellent ... wonderfully informative ... if you were on the team, you'd be absolutely fabulous, I'm sure of it ... you're not on the team.'[12] In the condescending environment of the male domain, if a man is in charge, a woman's work may be greeted with much insincere praise, but little in the way of rewards where it really counts – in the paycheque and on the promotion ladder.

Nor does a patronising pat on the back do much to motivate women devalued in this way by their superiors, further research showed. In a cunning reversal of the original experiment, male and female participants were put in the role of lowly team member, given feedback and allocated team positions by a (fictitious) male team leader. Then the participants worked their way through as many of the maths and reasoning problems as they could.

The women were clearly just as able as the men at solving these problems. They scored every bit as well as the men regardless of whether the feedback given to them had been rather cool or pleasantly enthusiastic, and with no regard to where on the team totem pole they had been placed. There was only one exception to this equality of performance between the sexes. This was when the team leader didn't match his magnanimous praise with a good spot on the team. In men, this had the effect of spurring them on to exceptional mental whizzery. The researchers suggest that, infuriated by the patronising injustice, the men directed their angry energy towards proving the team leader wrong. Curiously though, the same scenario of unfairly low placement had the opposite effect upon women. Although they were every bit as furious as the men about being condescended to, afterwards their performance on the problems was noticeably lacklustre. The researchers suggest that, having learnt the sad lesson that sexism is rife and unconquerable, the women's anger left them feeling hopelessly ineffective.

As if all this weren't bad enough, stereotypes don't even need other people to do their dirty work for them. The grubby fingerprinting can be found directly on the members of stereotyped groups. A woman in a maths class, or a black student in an exam, must both perform under the threatening shadow of the stereotype of inferiority. The anxiety that this stereotype threat generates hampers their natural ability, and the stereotype is confirmed.[13] Rather surprisingly, the burden that stereotype threat brings to its bearer is remarkably easy to uncover. For instance, men sometimes outperform women at maths, particularly at very advanced levels. This has, of course, led to all sorts of claims about genetic differences in maths ability between men and women. Yet researchers interested in stereotype threat were able to magically close this gender gap (and no genetic modification required).[14] One group of university maths students was given a hard maths test. The men outperformed the women. But hold your smirks, fellas, and don't be too quick to draw conclusions. A second group of students was given exactly the same test, but the participants were told beforehand that gender differences had never been found in how men and women scored on this particular test. When the cloud of stereotype threat was dispersed in this way, the women did every bit as well as the men.

Indeed, offering a rare ray of hope in this field of research, it seems that revealing the truth about stereotype threat to vulnerable students can set them free of its foreboding presence. Women statistics students showed the usual below-par performance on a maths test, in comparison with men, when it was threateningly presented as a part of a study of gender differences in mathematical ability.[15] But another group of students was told beforehand about stereotype threat and its effects. The women were advised that, 'It's important to keep in mind that, if you are feeling anxious while taking this test, this anxiety could be the result of these negative stereotypes that are widely known in society and have nothing to do with your actual ability to do well on the test.' Teachers, take note. Enlightened in this way, the women did every bit as well as the men. Ongoing research suggests that the performance of black students, too, may be able to be bolstered in just the same way.[16]

And there is yet another way to level the playing field. It is not only the case that stereotypes about maths are damaging to women. Men normally benefit slightly from the culturally ingrained assumption that they are naturally superior to women, an effect called stereotype lift.[17] Men don't perform quite as well if you whip this booster seat out from under them by informing them that, on this occasion, their possession of certain masculine physical attributes won't help their performance.

By now, you should be developing a certain grudging awe for the number of ways in which stereotypes further themselves: the bigot goggles, the self-fulfilling prophecy, stereotype threat and stereotype lift. Yet, you may furtively wonder, is this enough to explain why stereotypes live on, if there really is no truth to them? I will leave discussion of the 'kernel of truth' hypothesis to more courageous writers.[18] However, bear in mind that so far we have seen only the stereotype's arsenal of attack: the ways in which it distorts our judgments and behaviour. The stereotype also enjoys a strong line of defence against people inconsiderate enough to challenge our bigoted expectations. As revealed in 'The Deluded Brain', we're rather prone to fiddling the statistics to fit our beliefs. We fall prey to illusory correlation, seeing links between groups of people and traits that fit a stereotype, but don't actually exist. Are menopausal women really bad-tempered grumps, for example? According to their stereotype they are but, as one study showed, illusory correlation has much to answer for in perpetuating this moody image.[19] People hugely overestimate how often they have seen menopausal women in a stink.

Another clever way to discount people who don't fit in with your stereotyped beliefs is to pop them into a little category all of their own. As we saw in 'The Pigheaded Brain', we have a remarkable capacity to make up explanations to back up anything we happen to believe. In just the same way, we seize on handy little details to explain away the generous Jew, or the assertive woman. We will claim, 'Oh, but she went to such a posh girls' school' (or,

'Oh, but she went to such a rough comprehensive'), to account conveniently for what seems to us to be unusual assertiveness in a woman, leaving us with no urge to update our stereotype.[20] In fact, if the person deviates enough from her stereotype, we don't even feel the need to justify ignoring the challenge that her existence presents. Her freakishness, in our eyes, is seen as grounds enough for dismissing her as a counter-example.[21]

This is all dispiriting enough. But there is even more depressing news for those who do not fit the stereotypical mould of their sex. Gender 'deviants' are at risk of far worse treatment than merely being rejected as irrelevant. For instance, women who venture outside the acceptable limits set by gender stereotypes invite backlash against themselves. Research suggests that there are very good reasons why a woman can't 'be more like a man'. In the psychology laboratory, women who do unusually well on a 'masculine' test have been shown to have their chance of winning a prize in a quiz sabotaged by others.[22] In a business setting, women who behave 'like men' by promoting a highly confident and competent image of themselves in an interview are judged to be less socially skilled than are men who behave just the same.[23] (Regrettably, there are also good reasons for a woman not to behave like a woman. Women who are more 'femininely' modest about their skills are seen as less competent.)[24] These backlash effects may well play an important part in encouraging women to toe the line. And so the oppressive stereotype marches on.

While women who break the rules get the stick, those who conform get the carrot. A kinder, gentler form of prejudice, benevolent sexism, eulogises the warm, caring, nurturing virtues of 'wonderful women' (without whom men would not be complete). The enticing charm of benevolent sexism is certainly preferable to the hostile variety, so it is perhaps not surprising that women across the world subscribe to this flattering image of their gender to almost the same extent as men do.[25] Yet its appeal is perilous, for the honeyed stereotype of empathic woman serves to psychologically offset the fact that men have most of the political and economic power. The message that men and women are 'complementary but equal', and that we all benefit from fulfilling our natural role in society, lends an 'equalitarian veneer' to an age-old prejudice.[26] This is why, perhaps, in the most sexist countries of the world, women cling even more desperately to the second-rate compensations of benevolent sexism.[27]

Unfortunately, of course, women do not even have to personally endorse this old-fashioned 'women are from Venus' ideology in order for it to affect them. Researchers asked men and women to rate how much certain qualities apply to men and to women, as a way of priming gender stereotypes.[28] Some had the benevolent stereotype of women primed. They were asked about stereotypically feminine positive qualities – being considerate, warm and moral, for example. Others judged men as opposed to women on supposedly male qualities (being assertive, competitive and ambitious, for instance).

The researchers then looked to see what effect the stereotype priming had had in terms of stifling or fanning fires in bellies regarding gender inequalities. The volunteers were asked how much they agreed or disagreed with statements such as, 'In general, relations between men and women are fair' and 'The division of labour in families generally operates as it should'. The findings exposed the dangerously co-opting effects of the wonderful women stereotype. Women who had not been exposed to this stereotype were quite adamant that women don't get a fair shot, that men don't pull their weight at home and that a radical restructuring of society was called for. (And this was despite the fact that the heroic stereotype of man as the go-get-em hunter of society had just been primed.) But women who, beforehand, had been reminded that stereotypical womanhood brings its own sweet compensations, were just as complacently accepting of the status quo as were men. Charmed into unwitting submission, women become complicit in their own subordination.

Stereotypes, as you will have gathered from this chapter so far, are powerful enemies of equality. But, surprising though it may now seem, we do have some control over their influence on our bigoted brains. We are actually quite capable of resisting their use. Unfortunately, however, we appear to switch our stereotypes on and off in whatever way best suits our egos. For example, if we are criticised by a woman or a black person, we use our negative stereotype of them to cast aspersions on their judgment. By disparaging them in this way, we protect our vain brains from the hurtful effects of negative feedback.[29] If, however, it is praise rather than criticism issuing forth from a female or black mouth, we miraculously manage to inhibit our negative stereotypes, and consider our evaluators to be as able as any white man at their job. As the researchers of these studies succinctly put it,

'She's fine if she praised me but incompetent if she criticised me.'

Worse still, there is evidence that we will use stereotypes to disparage anyone we can in order to make ourselves feel better, even if it was not the slandered person who made us feel bad in the first place. Researchers cast a blow to the self-esteem of half of a group of students by telling them that they had scored lower than average on an intelligence test.[30] The other students were told that they had done extremely well. Some of the ego-bruised students were then given an opportunity to jolly themselves up at someone else's expense, using a negative stereotype. All the students were asked to evaluate a job candidate. Each of them considered the very same woman, and she appeared identical in each of her interviews, in all respects but one. For some of the students she was 'Julie Goldberg', volunteer for a Jewish organi-sation, member of a Jewish sorority and wearer of a Star of David necklace. To the other students she was presented as 'Maria D'Agostino', volunteer for a Catholic organisation, member of a European sorority, who bore a cross around her neck. This prob-ably requires no further spelling out, except to say that the researchers reported that the unflattering stereotype of the 'Jewish American Princess' was well known and widely discussed on the campus at which they ran this experiment. The students were, however, good enough not to hold anything in particular against Italian women.

The researchers were most interested in the students who, still reeling from their supposed inferiority on the intelligence test, were given the opportunity to perform the psychological equiv-alent of kicking the cat by being given a Jewish woman job applicant to evaluate. Could they be so ignoble as to deprecate this innocent woman, simply because their own noses had been put out of joint? They certainly could. Their ratings of the interviewee's personality and qualifications were far lower than everyone else's. But as cat-kickers everywhere will know, it certainly had the desired effect: their self-esteem went shooting up afterwards.

To be fair to our bigoted brains, people who want to avoid prejudiced thoughts can, and do, quash the activity of their stereotypes. However, this requires no small amount of mental effort. This means that if you are tired, distracted or under pressure, the stereotype can shake free of this restraint, returning to freedom to wreak its malignant influence.[31] When American researchers asked students to rate racist jokes using a Ha!Ha!-ometer, the students were suitably grudging with their Ha!Ha!'s. Yet students who were distracted while they rated the jokes (they had to do a demanding counting and memory task at the same time) found the racist jokes much funnier.[32] We lower our guard, too, if we feel that we have already established our egalitarian credentials. For example, people who are given the chance to flaunt their feminist stripes by rejecting blatantly sexist statements will then sit back and rest on their laurels. These quietly complacent people are subsequently more likely to agree with subtly sexist statements.[33]

Indeed, research suggests that even successful attempts to stem our prejudices can backfire later. We hold the stereotype down temporarily, but it bobs right back up again with increased vigour. Researchers asked people to write a day-in-the-life story about someone in a photo, who happened to be a skinhead.[34]

Some of the volunteers were asked to try to avoid stereotyping in their story. These volunteers did successfully suppress the skinhead stereotype; their stories contained far less material along the stereotypic lines of '… and then I thumped him one' and the like. However, the stereotype actually gained new strength from its brief confinement. Thanks to the unfortunate side effect of the way that our brains exert mental control (the ironic process theory we came across in 'The Weak-willed Brain'), repressed thoughts are actually primed by the mental butler. As a result, once our guard is down, these very thoughts are more likely to leap into consciousness. When the volunteers were asked shortly afterwards to write a second passage about a skinhead, their stories contained far more stereotyping than those of people who had been left to respond naturally to their stereotypes. The rebounding of the skinhead stereotype also showed its influence when the volunteers were invited to step into a room to meet the very skinhead whose photo they had seen. The skinhead wasn't there, but his belongings were on one of the chairs. People whose skinhead stereotypes were acting with fresh force (after being damped down in the day-in-the-life task) showed their heightened disdain and fear of the skinhead by choosing to sit further away from his belongings.

Does this mean that even the Equal Opportunities lawyer, after a hard day battling for equality in the workplace, is eventually worn down by omnipotent stereotypes? Does he clutch his briefcase more closely to his side when a black man sits next to him on the bus and, once home, berate his wife for not having dinner ready on the table? The outlook, fortunately, may not be quite this bleak.

People who sincerely wish to avoid stereotyping a particular group seem to be able to avoid the rebound effect that suppressing a stereotype usually brings. This motivation might be lacking in most people when it comes to skinheads, but strong enough (in at least some people) to keep less socially acceptable stereotypes about black, Asian or gay people at bay for longer. But again, we can do this only when we are mentally completely on our toes.[35]

This has been a discouraging story so far and it would be understandable if, at this point, you were to lay down the book and weep. The problem is that we need the efficiency that schemas buy us. Schemas provide a quick means of extracting and interpreting information from the complicated world around us, of forming useful generalisations, and making helpful predictions. A bigoted brain is an efficient brain. A brain unburdened by egalitarian concerns can decide 'Thug … tart … slob … nerd … airhead', then move swiftly on to the next thing on its 'To Do' list.[36] Yet this speed comes at the cost – mostly to others – of accuracy, particularly when our schemas fail to reflect reality truthfully. We don't always have (or make available) the time, opportunity, motivation or mental resources we need to consider the rich, complex and unique personalities of everyone we encounter. Nor do we always have the time or the inclination to pause to consider whether we are in peril of being prejudiced, and attempt to compensate for it. We may not even recognise the henchmen – or women – of stereotypes when they are staring us in the face. So ubiquitous is the image of women as sex objects, for example, that the researchers in the priming experiment of women as sex objects found, during debriefing, that many of the men who watched the sexist adverts were adamant that they must have been in the control group because the ads they saw 'weren't sexist'.

However, social psychologists are beginning to explore which strategies might help us thwart the bigoted tendencies of our brains.[37] The fact that our unconscious will eventually help out if we consistently make the conscious effort to act in a certain way in particular types of situation – the phenomenon described in 'The Secretive Brain' – offers a glimmer of hope. For it seems that we may be able to train our brain to replace its spontaneous prejudices with more acceptable reflexes.

The first step is to acknowledge your brain's unwelcome bigotry. And indeed, most of us are familiar with the disconcerting experience of a shamefully bigoted thought popping into our consciousness unbidden. A white person might know that he *shouldn't* feel especially worried about the intentions of a black man walking towards him on an empty street, yet in truth know that he probably would. When American researchers asked a group of non-black students about the differences between their 'should' and 'would' responses to black people, most admitted that they often experienced involuntary racist thoughts that were at odds with their consciously held colour-blind principles.

Yet a subset of the group claimed to almost always respond to black people as a good egalitarian should. You might think that they were deceiving themselves, or were perhaps trying to fake good to the researchers. But in fact, they seemed to have actually managed to reprogram their bigoted brains for the better. When the researchers gave these students the joke-rating task described earlier, the students remained unamused by the racist jokes, even when they were heavily distracted while they were making their Ha!Ha! ratings. Since their brains were too busy with the attention-grabbing counting and memorising to have been able to do much work suppressing any involuntary amusement at the racist jokes, these students must have been effortlessly disdainful of humour based on black stereotypes. From interviewing people with 'would' responses to black people that remained firmly in line with their 'shoulds', the researchers were inclined to think that these exemplary individuals had managed to rid themselves of their unwanted automatic prejudices through conscious effort and rehearsal.

If this sounds a little too daunting, a trusty implementation intention (one of the aides to the will we met in the 'The Weak-willed Brain') may offer an easier alternative for situations in which we know ourselves to be guilty of stereotyping. ('Whenever I see a Scottish person, I tell myself, "Don't stereotype!"' could be the rallying cry of my husband when next he catches a glimpse of tartan.) Researchers have found that people who form egalitarian implementation intentions of this sort are happily impervious to the usual unconscious effects of stereotype priming.[38]

This, then, gives us all something to strive towards. We can be slightly cheered by the thought that – with unceasing vigilance, constant practice and strenuous mental exertion – we might come to treat others fairly and justly in at least a few of the many situations that invite stereotyping. However, it is likely to be a longer and more arduous walk to freedom from bigotry than many of us are able to withstand.

Particularly in a Scottish bed and breakfast without a nice strong cup of tea to fortify us.

Epilogue: The Vulnerable Brain

So what are we to make of ourselves now? Through the course of this book, we've seen that the brain that we trust so implicitly to do the right thing by us has a mind of its own. An adroit manipulator of information, it leaves us staring at a mere façade of reality. Vanity shields us from unpalatable truths about ourselves. Craven methods of moral bookkeeping also attentively serve the principle of self-glorification, often at others' expense. The emotions add a misleading gloss of their own, colouring and confusing our opinions while unobtrusively masterminding our behaviour and sense of being. Irrationality clouds our judgment, leaving us vulnerable to errors and delusions – a situation that is only worsened by our pigheadedness. The secretive unconscious delights in a handful of strings to pull, concealing from us many of the true influences on our thoughts and deeds. Our very own will, temperamental and capricious, weakly succumbs to unwanted impulses and distractions. And, careless of our good intentions, the brain's ignoble use of stereotypes blurs our view of others to an all but inevitable bigotry.

Being confronted with the evidence of the distorting and deceptive window-dressings of the brain is unsettling, and rightly so. A brain with a mind of its own belies our strong sense that the world is just as it seems to us, and our misguided belief that our vision of 'out there' is sharp and true. In fact, it appears that our attitudes are the muddled outcome of many struggling factors. Tussling against our desire to know the truth about the world are powerful drives to protect our self-esteem, sense of security and pre-existing point of view. Set against our undeniably impressive powers of cognition is a multitude of irrationalities, biases and quirks that surreptitiously undermine the accuracy of our beliefs.

Little wonder we can't all get along! You may think that you are doing nothing more than skimming through the newspaper on the way to work but, as we now know, your mind is up to far more than you could ever have imagined. A report that divorce rates are on the increase is critically dismissed by the woman whose engagement ring sparkles bright and new.[1] 'No smoke without fire', is the confident view of the man furtively acquainting himself with the dying embers of a celebrity scandal in the society pages.[2] And reports headlined 'NO WEAPONS OF MASS DESTRUCTION FOUND IN IRAQ' leave at least some Americans believing that, well, weapons of mass destruction *were* found in Iraq.[3] In a striking real-world demonstration of the vulnerability of beliefs to the psychological context, Americans and Germans were asked to look closely at some news items from the Iraq war that were subsequently retracted. Germans (who as a country opposed the war) expressed great suspicion as to the coalition's true motives for war. (The word 'oil' did not go unmentioned.) Working from this distrustful frame of mind, they sensibly discounted misinformation about the war: as you would expect, they didn't believe things they knew to have been retracted. And almost none of the sceptical Germans wrongly recalled that weapons of mass destruction (WMD) had been discovered in Iraq.

But by way of bizarre contrast, Americans – even though they remembered that the statements about the war had later been retracted – still continued to believe them! And it was surely no coincidence that – with the destruction of WMD put forward as the primary motive for the US-led war – fully a third of the American sample succumbed to a false memory of that oft-spoken-of armoury. Thus, in their minds, the official US line regarding the necessity of war was thoroughly vindicated. Truth – already a casualty of war – received a second hard blow.

The mendacious mind doesn't just corrupt our view of the world: it also distorts our impression of other people. A judge in a small town in Pennsylvania, still mourning the loss of a family pet, comes down unduly hard on a defendant charged with cruelty to animals.[4] The psychiatrist, rattled by the incurable and devastating symptoms of children with autism, thinks it obvious that the parenting style of the wrecked and exhausted mothers must be to blame.[5] The passer-by wonders why the beggar doesn't pull himself together and get a job, without a thought to how circumstances and ill-fortune can drain willpower, and smother the best of intentions.[6] Meanwhile, the stereotypes with which we interpret the behaviour of others are constantly at work: simplifying, twisting, discounting and inventing. The wife, seething with fury at an injustice, is asked why she is so 'upset'.[7] The female scientist is judged 'not quite up to scratch' by her peers.[8] The black man fumbling for his wallet is shot dead by police.[9]

Nor is it just our understanding of others that is skewed and unreliable: it has been just as troubling, perhaps, to learn of the farce that passes for self-knowledge. Our conception of ourselves, we have discovered, is ever changing, fluidly adapting itself to our circumstances and moods, and the petulant demands of self-esteem. Nor does the devious brain always do us the courtesy of informing us of all the true sources of our feelings and views. What a shameful catalogue of arbitrary influences it has been. Despondency about your job, however heartfelt, will clear with the skies. *Joie de vivre* will be found together with that twenty-pound note on the street. The disliked work colleague seems less objectionable, thanks to the fragrant aroma of the new office air freshener.[10] One brand of spaghetti, rather than another, is thrown into your trolley because of where it is placed on the supermarket shelf.[11] And, as if psychologists had not embarrassed us enough already, they have recently revealed that we are strangely drawn towards those things that unconsciously remind us of the person we love above all others – ourselves. Blinded by self-love, when the brain assesses potential locales, careers and life-partners, it favours those that share the beloved letters that appear in your own name.[12] There are more people called Louis living in St. Louis than we would expect by chance. A dentist is more likely to be called Denis or Denise than (the equally popular) Jarrod or Beverly. Joseph is more likely to go down on bended knee before Josephine than Charlotte. ('How do I love thee? Let me count the Js', quip the researchers). Yet have you ever heard anyone explain that he moved to Seattle because his name is Sean? Even as we make some of the most important decisions of our lives, we are being unwittingly swayed by the brain's capricious concerns.

Little surprise, then, that the true motives for our actions remain disturbingly obscure much of the time. We appear to have as little insight into our own behaviour as we do our thoughts. Nor do we enjoy as much control over ourselves as we might once have believed. It is not only that conscious will is weak and truculent (and, perhaps, nothing more than a pleasing illusion). We have learned of some of the myriad ways in which, without our knowing a thing about it, our behaviour is subtly altered by what is going on around us. We are, to some extent, at the mercy of whatever schemas are primed within us. The filthy, unkempt train encourages even more careless treatment by its passengers.[13] The men's magazine filled with pictures of disrobed women leaves its readers more inclined to leer and flirt with their female companions.[14] The racist lyrics of the rap song playing on the radio kindle hostility against black people. Nor are we immune to the influences of the company we keep. Recent research has unearthed the contagion of other people's motivations. Men, exposed to a description of another man who tried to seduce a young woman into a casual sexual encounter, pursued this goal themselves with heightened vigour.[15]

What is most alarming about all of this research is how these imperceptible changes in us occur without our conscious permission. The man with even the most praiseworthy attitude towards women is susceptible to the subtle effects of the sexist billboards that bombard him on his way to work. The woman who clutches her head in her hands at the sight of John Gray's latest bestseller is nonetheless left a little less indignant about women's lot after laughing at a joke that exploits those very same Mars-versus-Venus caricatures of the genders. When the aggressive bad guy in the action movie is black, even the sincere subscriber to 'colour-blind' principles becomes triggered to misconstrue the intent of the black man who stops him to ask the time. Our values and principles offer scant defence against the insidious effects of our environment.

The remarkable exposés of the mind described in this book underline the importance of experimental psychology for our understanding of the world, other people and ourselves. It is difficult, if not impossible, to point the finger at a single person and, with any degree of certainty, charge them with the crime of bias. Real-life situations are too complicated for us to be able to say, 'You only think that parent should have custody of the child because of the way the question was phrased', or 'You gave that employee a smaller bonus because she's a woman', or 'You only chose that car because the car dealer plied you with free coffee and pastries'. Indeed, thanks to our illusory sense of self-knowledge, these claims (particularly if levelled at ourselves) seem ludicrous. But as we have seen, the well-designed psychology experiment – by carefully manipulating the factor of interest – can expose concrete and undeniable evidence of these strange and often unwelcome influences at work.

On a more hopeful note, recognising and acknowledging our vulnerability to the many common machinations of the brain provides modest scope to guard against them. Some sources of 'mental contamination' can be side-stepped by simple avoidance.[16]

If you don't want to take on the values of women's magazines unconsciously – don't buy them. If you don't want to be biased by racist expectations of how your black students will perform – mark papers anonymously. If you don't want distractedly to believe the trumped-up claims of adverts – don't watch them.[17] And if you don't want your children unconsciously taking on board violent, sexist, racist or grossly acquisitive messages from their environment, then avoid exposing your young ones to them whenever you can – and complain about them.

It is also a pleasure to inform you that, simply by reading this book, you have lightly armoured yourself against attacks on the integrity of your judgments and behaviour. (Why not protect your friends and family too? Buy them all their own copy.) Mental events that manipulate our brains – emotions, moods, schemas and stereotypes, and so on – lose some of their effect when we are aware of their potential to influence us. Remember the experiment described in 'The Emotional Brain', in which volunteers were asked about their life satisfaction on rainy or sunny days?[18] People asked about the weather beforehand were less affected by weather-induced mood when giving their ratings than were volunteers not alerted to the current climatic conditions. Of course, the notorious British propensity for using the weather as an opening conversational gambit should offer protection against this particular influence on our thoughts. But still, remaining mindful of our susceptibility to polluting influences can only help compensate against them. (Unfortunately, we don't always get this quite right; we sometimes under- or over-compensate. Still, it's better than nothing.)[19]

While the veil our brain stealthily drapes over reality can never be whipped away entirely, there are other reasons for us not to be completely disheartened. We can be encouraged by the fact that determined efforts on our part to see the world accurately can help counteract distortion. If precision is important enough to us, we are capable of greater conscientiousness in gathering and considering our evidence. If it is important enough to you not to stereotype a particular group, for example, then with not a little effort you will succeed, as we saw in 'The Bigoted Brain'. Nor, fortunately, must we be completely reliant on people motivating themselves to remove their bigot goggles. Making people accountable for their judgments of others goes a long way towards focusing their vision of other people with greater clarity.[20]

Best of all, we can recruit the brain's freelance mind to use to our own advantage, as when we consciously train the mental butler of our unconscious efficiently and effortlessly to fulfil our aspirations. With some exertion on our part, the unconscious can come to automatically respond to certain situations in a manner that is in line with our conscious wishes. Vigilant weight-watchers, described in 'The Weak-willed Brain', for example, trained their mental butlers to respond to calorific temptations with an instant pursing of the lips and a shake of the head. Similarly, as we saw in 'The Bigoted Brain', it seems possible for us to cajole our brain into replacing its unwanted illiberal reactions to stereotyped groups with more enlightened attitudes.

Yet with this faint hope, that we are not entirely defenceless martyrs to the fictions of the brain, comes responsibility. 'Wisdom is the principal thing; therefore get wisdom; and with all thy getting, get understanding.' This is no simple matter, of course. It is far easier to apply the lessons of the research described here to others than to oneself.[21] Ironically, it is part-and-parcel of the vanities and weaknesses of the human brain that we secretly doubt that we ourselves are vulnerable to those vanities and weaknesses. (I asked my husband if he felt that I had become a more tolerant, understanding and perceptive person since writing this book. He stared at me blankly.)

However, let us rise loftily above ourselves. We owe a duty both to ourselves and to others to lessen the harmful effects of the brain's various shams whenever we can. To be all eyes and ears for influences that may lead us astray when we are making important decisions. To be more tolerant of opposing viewpoints, however much it may seem that we are on the side of the angels. To bolster our feeble wills against temptations, distractions and impulses. To resist the easy complicity of stereotypes when judging others. To endeavour to put in the necessary groundwork to bring the unruly actions of the unconscious in line with our principles and values. And not to exploit the loose leash of other people's brains in order to sell more soft drinks.

Above all, we should try to remain alert always to the distortions and deceptions of our wayward brains. For they are always with us.

Notes and References

Chapter 1: The Vain Brain

1 J.M. Nuttin (1985), 'Narcissism beyond Gestalt and awareness: the name-letter effect', *European Journal of Social Psychology*, 15: 353–61.

2 For example, N. Epley and D. Dunning (2000), 'Feeling "holier than thou": Are self-serving assessments produced by errors in self- or social prediction?', *Journal of Personality and Social Psychology*, 79: 861–75; C. Heath (1999), 'On the social psychology of agency relationships: lay theories of motivation overemphasize extrinsic incentives', *Organizational Behavior & Human Decision Processes*, 78: 25–62; O. Svenson (1981), 'Are we all less risky and more skillful than our fellow drivers?', *Acta Psychologica*, 47: 143–8.

3 D. Dunning, J. A. Meyerowitz and A. D. Holzberg (2002), 'Ambiguity and self-evaluation: the role of idiosyncratic trait definition in self-serving assessments of ability', in T. Gilovich et al. (eds), *Heuristics and biases: the psychology of intuitive judgment*, New York, NY: Cambridge University Press (pp. 324–33).

4 For example, when considering what makes an intelligent or creative person, or a good leader, people regard the attributes that they themselves possess as the most important. D. Dunning, M. Perie and A. L. Story (1991), 'Self-serving prototypes of social categories', *Journal of Personality and Social Psychology*, 16: 957–68.

5 J. D. Campbell (1986), 'Similarity and uniqueness: the effects of attribute type, relevance, and individual differences in self-esteem and depression', *Journal of Personality and Social Psychology*, 50: 281–94.

6 For example, J. R. Larson (1977), 'Evidence for a self-serving bias in the attribution of causality', *Journal of Personality*, 45: 430–41.

7   W. K. Campbell and C. Sedikides (1999), 'Self-threat magnifies the self-serving bias: A meta-analytic integration', *Review of General Psychology*, 3: 23–43.

8   E. Pronin D. Y. Lin and L. Ross (2002), 'The bias blind spot: perceptions of bias in self versus others', *Personality and Social Psychology Bulletin*, 28: 369–81.

9   L. J. Sanna and E. C. Chang (2003), 'The past is not what it used to be: optimists' use of retroactive pessimism to diminish the sting of failure', *Journal of Research in Personality*, 37: 388–404.

10 T. W. Smith, C. R. Snyder and M. M. Handelsman (1982), 'On the self-serving function of an academic wooden leg: test anxiety as a self-handicapping strategy', *Journal of Personality and Social Psychology*, 42: 314–21.

11 J. M. Burger and R. M. Huntzinger (1985), 'Temporal effects on attributions for one's own behavior: the role of task outcome', *Journal of Experimental Social Psychology*, 21: 247–61.

12 C. Sedikides and J. D. Green (2000), 'On the self-protective nature of inconsistency-negativity management: using the person memory paradigm to examine self-referent memory', *Journal of Personality and Social Psychology*, 79: 906–22.

13 H. Markus and E. Wurf (1987), 'The dynamic self-concept: A social psychological perspective', *Annual Review of Psychology*, 38: 299–337.

14 Z. Kunda and R. Sanitioso (1989), 'Motivated changes in the self-concept', *Journal of Experimental Social Psychology*, 25: 272–85.

15 R. Sanitioso, Z. Kunda and G. T. Fong (1990), 'Motivated recruitment of autobiographical memories', *Journal of Personality and Social Psychology*, 59: 229–41.

16 R. Sanitioso and R. Wlordarski (2004), 'In search of information that confirms a desired self-perception: motivated processing of social feedback and choice of social interactions', *Personality and Social Psychology Bulletin*, 30: 412–22.

17 The 'intuitive lawyer' versus the 'intuitive scientist' styles of information processing are contrasted by R. F. Baumeister and L. S. Newman (1994), 'Self-regulation of cognitive inference and decision processes',

Personality and Social Psychology Bulletin, 20: 3–19.

18 Z. Kunda (1987), 'Motivated inference: self-serving generation and evaluation of causal theories', *Journal of Personality and Social Psychology*, 53: 636–47.

19 R. S. Wyer and D. Frey (1983), 'The effects of feedback about self and others on the recall and judgments of feedback-relevant information', *Journal of Experimental Social Psychology*, 19: 540–59.

20 For summary, see Z. Kunda (1990), 'The case for motivated reasoning', *Psychological Bulletin*, 108: 480–98.

21 R. Sanitioso and R. Wlordarski (2004), 'In search of information that confirms a desired self-perception: motivated processing of social feedback and choice of social interactions', *Personality and Social Psychology Bulletin*, 30: 412–22.

22 Z. Kunda (1987), 'Motivated inference: self-serving generation and evaluation of causal theories', *Journal of Personality and Social Psychology*, 53: 636–47.

23 P. H. Ditto and D. F. Lopez (1992), 'Motivated skepticism: use of differential decision criteria for preferred and nonpreferred conclusions', *Journal of Personality and Social Psychology*, 63: 568–84.

24 G. A. Quattrone and A. Tversky (1984), 'Causal versus diagnostic contingencies: on self-deception and on the voter's illusion', *Journal of Personality and Social Psychology*, 46: 237–48.

25 C. R. Snyder (1978), 'The "illusion" of uniqueness', *Journal of Humanistic Psychology*, 18: 33–41.

26 Z. Kunda (1987), 'Motivated inference: self-serving generation and evaluation of causal theories', *Journal of Personality and Social Psychology*, 53: 636–47.

27 For a brief review of the 'Illusions of control' and when it occurs, see S. C. Thompson (1999), 'Illusions of control: how we overestimate our personal control', *Current Directions in Psychological Science*, 8: 187–90.

28 P. M. Biner, S. T. Angle, J. H. Park, A. E. Mellinger and B. C. Barber (1995), 'Need and the illusion of control', *Personality and Social Psychology Bulletin*, 21: 899–907.

29 For example, see E. Babad (1997), 'Wishful thinking among voters: motivational and cognitive influences', *International Journal of Public Opinion Research*, 9: 105–25.

30 E. Babad and Y. Katz (1991), 'Wishful thinking – against all odds', *Journal of Applied Social Psychology*, 21: 1921–38.

31 C. J. Uhlaner and B. Grofman (1986), 'The race may be close but my horse is going to win: Wish fulfillment in the 1980 presidential election', *Political Behavior*, 8: 101–29.

32 E. Babad (1997), 'Wishful thinking among voters: motivational and cognitive influences', *International Journal of Public Opinion Research*, 9: 105–25.

33 P. C. Price (2000), 'Wishful thinking in the prediction of competitive outcomes', *Thinking and Reasoning*, 6: 161–72.

34 S. E. Taylor and J. D. Brown (1988), 'Illusion and well-being: a social psychological perspective on mental health', *Psychological Bulletin*, 103: 193–210.

35 For a readable account of Martin Seligman's research on explanatory style, see R. J. Trotter (1987), 'Stop blaming yourself', *Psychology Today*, 21: 31–9.

36 D. D. Danner, D. A. Snowdon and W. V. Friesen (2001), 'Positive emotions in early life and longevity: findings from the nun study', *Journal of Personality and Social Psychology*, 80: 804–13.

37 From comparing the lowest and highest quartiles on number of positive emotion words, and number of different positive emotions expressed in the passage.

38 B. L. Fredrickson and R. W. Levenson (1998), 'Positive emotions speed recovery from the cardiovascular sequelae of negative emotions', *Cognition and Emotion*, 12: 191–220.

39 S. C. Segerstrom, S. E. Taylor, M. E. Kemeny and J. J. Fahey (1998), 'Optimism is associated with mood, coping, and immune change in response to stress', *Journal of Personality and Social Psychology*, 74: 1646–55.

40 See C. R. Snyder and R. L. Higgins (1988), 'Excuses: their effective role in the negotiation of reality', *Psychological Bulletin*, 104: 23–35.

41 R. Buehler, D. Griffin and M. Ross (1994), 'Exploring the "Planning Fallacy": why people underestimate their task completion times', *Journal of Personality and Social Psychology*, 67: 366–81.

42 M. Fenton-O'Creeny, N. Nicholson, E. Soane and P. Willman (2003), 'Trading on illusions: Unrealistic perceptions of control and trading performance', *Journal of Occupational and Organizational Psychology* 76: 53–68.

43 Salary decrease referred to in text refers to the effect on annual remuneration of one standard deviation change in 'illusion of control' score, according to the regression coefficient.

44 As assessed using questionnaire measures. S. E. Taylor and P. M. Gollwitzer (1995), 'Effects of mindset on positive illusions', *Journal of Personality and Social Psychology*, 69: 213–26. And P. M. Gollwitzer and R. F. Kinney (1989), 'Effects of deliberative and implemental mind-sets on illusion of control', *Journal of Personality and Social Psychology*, 56: 531–42.

45 See S. E. Taylor and J. D. Brown (1988), 'Illusion and well-being: a social psychological perspective on mental health', *Psychological Bulletin*, 103: 193–210.

46 R. K. Deppe and J. M. Harackiewicz (1996), 'Self-handicapping and intrinsic motivation: buffering intrinsic motivation from the threat of failure', *Journal of Personality and Social Psychology*, 70: 868–76.

47 C. S. Dweck (1975), 'The role of expectations and attributions in the alleviation of learned helplessness', *Journal of Personality and Social Psychology*, 31: 674–85; M. Chapin and D. G. Dyck (1976), 'Persistence in children's reading behavior as a function of N length and attribution retraining', *Journal of Abnormal Psychology*, 85: 511–15.

48 T. D. Wilson and P. W. Linville (1985), 'Improving the performance of college freshmen with attributional techniques', *Journal of Personality and Social Psychology*, 49: 287–93.

49 T. Pyszczynski, J. Greenberg, S. Solomon, J. Arndt and J. Schimel (2004), 'Why do people need self-esteem? A theoretical and empirical review', *Psychological Bulletin*, 130: 435–68.

CHAPTER 2: The Emotional Brain

1   A. Bechara, H. Damasio and A. R. Damasio (2000), 'Emotion, decision making and the orbitofrontal cortex', *Cerebral Cortex*, 10: 295–307.

2   P. J. Eslinger and A. R. Damasio (1985), 'Severe disturbance of higher cognition after bilateral frontal lobe ablation: Patient EVR', *Neurology*, 35: 1731–41.

3   J. L. Saver and A. R. Damasio (1991), 'Preserved access and processing of social knowledge in a patient with acquired sociopathy due to ventromedial frontal damage', *Neuropsychologia*, 29: 1241–9.

4   A. R. Damasio, D. Tranel and H. Damasio (1990), 'Individuals with sociopathic behavior caused by frontal damage fail to respond autonomically to social stimuli', *Behavioral Brain Research*, 41: 81–94.

5   A. Bechara, H. Damasio and A. R. Damasio (2000), 'Emotion, decision making and the orbitofrontal cortex', *Cerebral Cortex*, 10: 295–307.

6   For discussion of role of arousal in emotion, see G. Mandler (1984), *Mind and emotion: psychology of emotion and stress*, New York: W. W. Norton.

7   A. F. Ax (1953), 'The physiological differentiation between fear and anger in humans', *Psychosomatic Medicine*, 15: 433–42.

8   According to G. Mandler (1984), *Mind and emotion: psychology of emotion and stress*, New York: W. W. Norton.

9   J. R. Cantor, D. Zillman and J. Bryant (1975), 'Enhancement of experienced sexual arousal in response to erotic stimuli through misattribution of unrelated residual excitation', *Journal of Personality and Social Psychology*, 32: 69–75.

10 N. Schwartz, F. Strack, D. Kommer and D. Wagner (1987), 'Soccer, rooms, and the quality of your life: mood effects on judgments of satisfaction with life in general and with specific domains', *European Journal of Social Psychology*, 17: 69–79; E. J. Johnson and A. Tversky (1983), 'Affect, generalization, and the perception of risk', *Journal of Personality and Social Psychology*, 45: 20–31; L. M. Isbell and R. S. Wyer (1999), 'Correcting for mood-induced bias in the evaluation

of political candidates: the role of intrinsic and extrinsic motivation', *Personality and Social Psychology Bulletin*, 25: 237–49.

11 A. M. Isen, T. E. Shalker, M. Clark and L. Karp (1978), 'Affect, accessibility of material in memory, and behavior: a cognitive loop?', *Journal of Personality and Social Psychology*, 36: 1–12.

12 N. Schwartz and G. L. Clore (1983), 'Mood, misattribution, and judgments of well-being: informative and directive functions of affective states', *Journal of Personality and Social Psychology*, 45: 513–23.

13 C. Villemure, B. M. Slotnick and M. C. Bushnell (2003), 'Effects of odors on pain perception: deciphering the roles of emotion and attention', *Pain*, 106: 101–8.

14 E. J. Johnson and A. Tversky (1983), 'Affect, generalization, and the perception of risk', *Journal of Personality and Social Psychology*, 45: 20–31; J. P. Forgas (1994), 'Sad and guilty? Affective influences on the explanation of conflict in close relationships', *Journal of Personality and Social Psychology*, 66: 56–68; V. M. Esses and M. P. Zanna (1995), 'Mood and the expression of ethnic stereotypes', *Journal of Personality and Social Psychology*, 69: 1052–68.

15 See, for example, J. P. Forgas (1995), 'Mood and judgment: the Affect Infusion Model (AIM)', *Psychological Bulletin*, 117: 39–66.

16 P. M. Niedenthal, J. B. Halberstadt, J. Margolin and A. H. Innes-Ker (2000), 'Emotional state and the detection of chance in facial expression of emotion', *European Journal of Social Psychology*, 30: 211–22.

17 R. H. Fazio, D. R. Roskos-Ewoldsen and M. C. Powell (1994), 'Attitudes, perception, and attention', in P. M. Niedenthal and S. Kitayama (eds), *The Heart's Eye: emotional influences in perception and attention*, San Diego: Academic Press (pp. 197–216).

18 See W. R. Walker, J. J. Skowronski and C. P. Thompson (2003). 'Life is pleasant – and memory helps to keep it that way!', *Review of General Psychology*, 7: 203–10.

19 See C. Senior, E. Hunter, M. V. Lambert et al. (2001), 'Depersonalisation', *The Psychologist*, 14: 128–32.

20 M. Sierra, C. Senior, J. Dalton et al. (2002), 'Autonomic response in

depersonalization disorder', *Archives of General Psychiatry*, 59: 833–38.

21 M. L. Phillips, N. Medford, C. Senior et al. (2001), 'Depersonalization disorder: thinking without feeling', *Psychiatry Research: Neuro-imaging Section*, 108: 145–60.

22 For reports of experiences of depersonalisation patients see, for example, S. Bockner (1949), 'The depersonalization syndrome: report of a case', *Journal of Mental Science*, 93: 968–71; G. Simeon, S. Gross and O. Guralnik (1997), 'Feeling unreal: 30 cases of DSM-III-R Depersonalization Disorder', *American Journal of Psychiatry*, 154: 1107–13.

23 One hypothesis is that background feelings contribute importantly to the sense of self. See A. R. Damasio (1996), *Descarte's error*, London: Macmillan.

24 See A. W. Young and K. Leafhead (1996), 'Betwixt life and death: case studies of the Cotard delusion', in P. W. Halligan and J. C. Marshall (eds), *Method in madness: case studies in cognitive neuro-psychiatry*, Hove, East Sussex: Psychology Press (pp. 147–71).

CHAPTER 3: The Immoral Brain

1 J. Haidt (2001), 'The emotional dog and its rational tail: a social intuitionist approach to moral judgment', *Psychological Review*, 108: 814–34.

2 J. Haidt and M. A. Hersh, M.A. (2001), 'Sexual morality: the cultures and emotions of conservatives and liberals', *Journal of Applied Social Psychology*, 31: 191–221.

3 J. S. Lerner, J. H. Goldberg and P. E. Tetlock (1998), 'Sober second thought: the effects of accountability, anger, and authoritarianism on attributions of responsibility', *Personality and Social Psychology Bulletin*, 24: 563–74.

4 M. J. Lerner (1980), *The belief in a just world: a fundamental delusion*, New York and London: Plenum Press.

5   See M. J. Lerner (1980), ibid; Also L. Montada and M. J. Lerner (1998), *Responses to victimizations and belief in a just world.* New York and London: Plenum Press.

6   See, for example, G. Younge (2005), 'Murder and rape – fact or fiction?', *The Guardian*, 6 September. Retrieved on 24 October 2005 from: http://www.guardian.co.uk/katrina/story/0,16441,1563532, 00.html

7   R. Buehler, D. Griffin and M. Ross (1994), 'Exploring the "Planning Fallacy": why people underestimate their task completion times', *Journal of Personality and Social Psychology*, 67: 366–81.

8   F. D. Fincham, S. R. Beach and D. H. Baucom (1987), 'Attribution processes in distressed and nondistressed couples: 4. Self-partner attribution differences', *Journal of Personality and Social Psychology*, 52: 739–48.

9   A. Schütz (1999), 'It was your fault! Self-serving biases in auto-biographical accounts of conflicts in married couples', *Journal of Social and Personal Relationships*, 16: 193–208.

10 F. D. Fincham, S. R. Beach and D. H. Baucom (1987), 'Attribution processes in distressed and nondistressed couples: 4. Self-partner attribution differences', *Journal of Personality and Social Psychology*, 52: 739–48.

11 A. Schütz (1999), 'It was your fault! Self-serving biases in auto-biographical accounts of conflicts in married couples', *Journal of Social and Personal Relationships*, 16: 193–208.

12 J. Kruger and T. Gilovich (2004), 'Actions, intentions, and self-assessment: the road to self-enhancement is paved with good intentions', *Personality and Social Psychology Bulletin*, 30: 328–39.

13 S. Milgram (1963), 'Behavioral study of obedience', *Journal of Abnormal and Social Psychology*, 67: 371–8.

14 E. Tarnow (2000), 'Self-destructive obedience in the airplane cockpit and the concept of obedience optimization', in T. Blass (ed), *Obedience to authority: Current perspectives on the Milgram paradigm*, Mahway, NJ: Lawrence Erlbaum Associates (pp. 111–23)

15 J. M. Darley and C. D. Batson (1973), '"From Jerusalem to Jericho":
    A study of situational and dipositional variables in helping behavior',
    Journal of Personality and Social Psychology, 27:100–19.
16 G. Geher, K. P. Bauman, S. E. K. Hubbard and J. R. Legare (2002),
    'Self and other obedience estimates: biases and moderators', *Journal
    of Social Psychology*, 142: 677–89.
17 On average, they saw themselves delivering nothing more powerful
    than about 140 volts, at the low end of the 'Strong Shock' category
    on Milgram's shock generator control panel.
18 See D. T. Gilbert and P. S. Malone (1995), 'The correspondence bias',
    Psychological Bulletin, 117: 21–38. The correspondence bias is also
    known as the fundamental attribution error.
19 M. A. Safer (1980), 'Attributing evil to the subject, not the situation:
    Student reaction to Milgram's film on obedience', *Personality and
    Social Psychology Bulletin*, 6: 205–09.
20 P. Pietromonaco and R. E. Nisbett (1982), 'Swimming upstream
    against the fundamental attribution error: Subjects' weak general-
    izations from the Darley and Batson study', *Social Behavior and
    Personality*, 10: 1–4.
21 A suggestion made by D. T. Gilbert and P. S. Malone (1995), 'The
    correspondence bias', *Psychological Bulletin*, 117: 21–38.
22 L. Festinger and J. M. Carlsmith (1959), 'Cognitive consequences of
    forced compliance', *Journal of Abnormal and Social Psychology*, 58:
    203–10.
23 A. M. Rosenthal (1999), *Thirty-eight witnesses: the Kitty Genovese
    case*, Berkeley, CA: University of California Press.
24 See C. R. Snyder (1985), 'Collaborative companions: the relationship
    of self-deception and excuse making', in M. W. Martin (ed), *Self-
    deception and self-understanding: new essays in philosophy and
    psychology*, Lawrence: University of Kansas Press (pp. 35–51).

CHAPTER 4: The Deluded Brain

1 The current diagnostic definition of delusion, according to the *Diagnostic and Statistical Manual IV*, is: 'a false belief based on incorrect inference about external reality that is firmly sustained despite what almost everyone else believes and despite what constitutes incontrovertible and obvious proof or evidence to the contrary' (American Psychiatric Association, 1994: p. 765). For discussion of difficulties in adequately defining delusions, see B.V. Halligan and H. Ellis (2003), 'Beliefs about delusions', *The Psychologist*, 16: 418–23.

2 See B.A. Maher (1999), 'Anomalous experience in everyday life: its significance for psychopathology', *The Monist*, 82: 547–70. Also E. Cardeña, S.J. Lynn and S. Krippner (eds), *Varieties of anomalous experience: examining the scientific evidence*, Washington, DC: American Psychological Association.

3 Z. Kunda, G.T. Fong, R. Sanitioso and E. Reber (1993), 'Directional questions direct self-conceptions', *Journal of Experimental Social Psychology*, 29: 63–86.

4 E. Shafir (1983), 'Choosing versus rejecting: why some options are both better and worse than others', *Memory and Cognition*, 21: 546–56.

5 L.J. Chapman and J.P. Chapman (1969), 'Illusory correlation as an obstacle to the use of valid diagnostic signs', *Journal of Abnormal Psychology*, 74: 271–80.

6 M. Conway and M. Ross (1984), 'Getting what you want by revising what you had', *Journal of Personality and Social Psychology*, 47: 738–48.

7 For a readable and comprehensive account of normal irrationality, see S. Sutherland (1994), *Irrationality: The enemy within*, London: Penguin.

8 For illuminating discussion on the power of expectations with regard to the 'Premenstrual Syndrome', see C. Tavris (1992), *The mismeasure of women: why women are not the better sex, the inferior sex, or the opposite sex*, New York: Touchstone.

9   See H. D. Ellis and M. B. Lewis (2001), 'Capgras delusion: a window on face recognition', *Trends in Cognitive Sciences*, 5: 149–56.

10 D. N. Anderson and E. Williams (1994), 'The delusion of inanimate doubles', *Psychopathology*, 27: 220–5.

11 H. D. Ellis, A. W. Young, A. H. Quayle and K. W. De Pauw (1997), 'Reduced autonomic responses to faces in Capgras delusion', *Proceedings of the Royal Society of London Series B, Biological Sciences*, 264: 1085–92.

12 H. D. Ellis and A. W. Young (1990), 'Accounting for delusional misidentifications', *British Journal of Psychiatry*, 157: 239–48.

13 For example, M. P. Alexander, D. T. Stuss and D. F. Benson (1979), 'Capgras syndrome: a reduplicative phenomenon', *Neurology*, 28: 334–9.

14 See, for example, P. A. Garety and D. Freeman (1999), 'Cognitive approaches to delusions: A critical review of theories and evidence', *British Journal of Clinical Psychology*, 38: 113–54.

15 P. A. Garety, D. R. Hemsley and S. Wessely (1991), 'Reasoning in deluded schizophrenic and paranoid patients: biases in performance on a probabilistic inference task', *The Journal of Nervous and Mental Disease*, 179: 194–201.

16 For criticisms of the 'jumping to conclusions' hypothesis, see B. A. Maher and M. Spitzer (1993), 'Delusions', in P. B. Sutker and H. E. Adams (eds), *Comprehensive handbook of psychopathology*, 2nd edn, New York: Plenum Press (pp. 263–93).

17 P. C. Wason and P. N. Johnson-Laird (1972), *Psychology of reasoning: Structure and content*. UK: BT Batsford (pp. 229–39).

18 For example, R. Kemp, S. Chua, P. McKenna and A. David (1997), 'Reasoning and delusions', *British Journal of Psychiatry*, 170: 398–405; R. P. Bentall and H. F. Young (1996), 'Sensible hypothesis testing in deluded, depressed and normal subjects', *British Journal of Psychiatry*, 168: 372–5.

19 These are the 'two-factor' models, for example, M. Davies, M. Coltheart, R. Langdon and N. Breen (2001), 'Monothematic delusions: Towards a two-factor account', *Philosophy, Psychiatry and Psychology*, 8: 133–58.

20 B. A. Maher (1999), 'Anomalous experience in everyday life: its significance for psychopathology', *The Monist*, 82: 547–70.

21 See P. G. Zimbardo (1999), 'Discontinuity theory: cognitive and social searches for rationality and normality – may lead to madness', in M. P. Zanna (ed), *Advances in Experimental Social Psychology*, 31: 345–486.

22 It should be noted that phobias are classified as anxiety disorders, rather than delusions. Delusional disorder: somatic type is the delusion that one has a physical defect or medical condition. Delusional disorder: persecutory type is the delusion that oneself (or someone close to you) is being treated malevolently.

23 C. D. Frith (1992), *The cognitive neuropsychology of schizophrenia*, Hove, UK: LEA.

24 Reported in B. A. Maher (1988), 'Anomalous experience and delusional thinking: the logic of explanations', in T. F. Oltmanns and B. A. Maher (eds), *Delusional beliefs*, New York: John Wiley and Sons.

25 E. R. Peters, S. A. Joseph and P. A. Garety (1999), 'Measurement of delusional ideation in the normal population: introducing the PDI (Peters et al. Delusions Inventory)', *Schizophrenia Bulletin*, 25: 553–76.

26 *Time*/CNN (15 June 1997), *Poll: U.S. hiding knowledge of aliens* [CNN Interactive poll posted on the internet], retrieved on 22 November 2004 from: http://www.cnn.com/US/9706/15/ufo.poll/index.html

27 E. R. Peters, S. A. Joseph and P. A. Garety (1999), 'Measurement of delusional ideation in the normal population: introducing the PDI (Peters et al. Delusions Inventory)', *Schizophrenia Bulletin*, 25: 553–76.

28 See S. Sanderson, B. Vandenberg and P. Paese (1999), 'Authentic religious experience or insanity?' *Journal of Clinical Psychology*, 55: 607–16; S. O'Connor and B. Vandenberg (2005), 'Psychosis or faith? Clinicians' assessments of religious beliefs', *Journal of Consulting and Clinical Psychology*, 73: 610–16. The overall ratings of psychotic pathology for Catholic beliefs were significantly lower than were those ratings for Mormon beliefs.

A MIND OF ITS OWN

29 Suggested by, for example, B. A. Maher (1999), 'Anomalous experience in everyday life: its significance for psychopathology', *The Monoist*, 82: 547–70.

30 For example, non-psychiatric patients who experience hallucinations are more likely to be married, to be happy to talk about their voices, and to have positive voice experiences, than psychiatric hallucinators. There don't appear to be great differences in the hallucinatory experiences per se. See R. P. Bentall (2000), 'Hallucinatory experiences', in E. Cardeña, S. J. Lynn and S. Krippner (eds), *Varieties of anomalous experience: examining the scientific evidence*, Washington, DC: American Psychological Association (pp. 85–120).

CHAPTER 5: The Pigheaded Brain

1 D. Sedaris (2004), *Dress your family in corduroy and denim*, London: Abacus.

2 T. R. Caretta and R. L. Moreland (1982), 'Nixon and Watergate: A field demonstration of belief perseverance', *Personality and Social Psychology Bulletin*, 8: 446–53.

3 A. J. Stewart, J. G. Webb, D. Giles and D. Hewitt (1956), 'Preliminary Communication: Malignant disease in childhood and diagnostic irradiation in utero', *Lancet*, 447. For details of Alice Stewart's research, see G. Greene (1999), *The woman who knew too much: Alice Stewart and the secrets of radiation*, Ann Arbor: University of Michigan Press.

4 C. G. Lord, L. Ross and M. R. Lepper (1979), 'Biased assimilation and attitude polarization: the effects of prior theories on subsequently considered evidence', *Journal of Personality and Social Psychology*, 37: 2098–109.

5 K. Edwards and E. E. Smith (1996), 'A disconfirmation bias in the evaluation of arguments', *Journal of Personality and Social Psychology*, 71: 5–24.

6 M. J. Mahoney (1977), 'Publication prejudices: an experimental study of confirmatory bias in the peer review system', *Cognitive Therapy and Research*, 1: 161–75.

7   Reported in G. Greene (1999), *The woman who knew too much: Alice Stewart and the secrets of radiation*, Ann Arbor: University of Michigan Press.

8   S.E. Taylor and Gollwitzer (1995), 'Effects of mindset on positive illusions', *Journal of Personality and Social Psychology*, 69: 213–26.

9   See M. Talbot (2000), 'The placebo prescription', *New York Times Magazine*, January 9, available at: http://www.nytimes.com/library/magazine/home/20000109mag-talbot7.html

10 F. Benedetti, G. Maggi and L. Lopiano (2003), 'Open versus hidden medical treatments: The patient's knowledge about a therapy affects the therapy outcome', *Prevention and Treatment*, 6.

11 See, for example, R. Rosenthal (2002), 'Experimenter and clinician effects in scientific inquiry and clinical practice', *Prevention and Treatment*, 5; R. Rosenthal (1994), 'Interpersonal expectancy effects: A 30-year perspective', *Current Directions in Psychological Science*, 3: 176–9.

12 R. Rosenthal (2003), 'Covert communication in laboratories, class-rooms and the truly real world', *Current Directions in Psychological Science*, 12: 151–4.

13 G. Downey, A.L. Freitas, B. Michaelis and H. Khouri (1998), 'The self-fulfilling prophecy in close relationships: rejection sensitivity and rejection by romantic partners', *Journal of Personality and Social Psychology*, 75: 545–60.

14 R.P. Abelson (1986), 'Beliefs are like possessions', *Journal for the Theory of Social Behaviour*, 16: 223–50.

15 L. Ross, M.R. Lepper and M. Hubbard (1975), 'Perseverance in self-perception and social perception: biased attributional processes in the debriefing paradigm', *Journal of Personality and Social Psychology*, 32: 880–92.

16 M.R. Lepper, L. Ross and R.R. Lau (1986), 'Persistence of inaccurate beliefs about the self: perseverance effects in the classroom', *Journal of Personality and Social Psychology*, 50: 482–91.

17 L. Ross, M.R. Lepper, F. Stack and J. Steinmetz (1977), 'Social explanation and social expectation: effects of real and hypothetical

explanations on subjective likelihood', *Journal of Personality and Social Psychology*, 35: 817–29.

18 D. T. Gilbert, R.W. Tafarodi and P. S. Malone (1993), 'You can't not believe everything you read', *Journal of Personality and Social Psychology*, 65: 221–33. See also D. T. Gilbert (1991), 'How mental systems believe', *American Psychologist*, 46: 107–19.

19 R. E. Petty and J. T. Cacioppo (1986), 'The elaboration likelihood model of persuasion', in L. Berkowitz (ed), *Advances in Experimental Social Psychology*, 19: 123–205.

20 D. T. Gilbert, R. W. Tafarodi and P. S. Malone (1993), 'You can't not believe everything you read', *Journal of Personality and Social Psychology*, 65: 221–33.

21 D. M. Wegner, R. Wenzlaff, R. M. Kerker and A. E. Beattie (1981), 'Incrimination through innuendo: can media questions become public answers?', *Journal of Personality and Social Psychology*, 40: 822–32.

22 For an explanation of this result, see D. T. Gilbert (1991), 'How mental systems believe', *American Psychologist*, 46: 107–19.

23 J. D. Lieberman and J. D. Arndt (2000), 'Understanding the limits of limiting instructions: social psychological explanations for the failures of instructions to disregard pretrial publicity and other inadmissible evidence', *Psychology, Public Policy and Law*, 6: 677–711.

24 F. B. Bryant and R. L. Guilbault (2002), '"I knew it all along" eventually: the development of hindsight bias in reaction to the Clinton impeachment verdict', *Basic and Applied Social Psychology*, 24: 27–41.

25 For review of the 'hindsight bias' effect, see S. A. Hawkins and R. Hastie (1990), 'Hindsight: biased judgments of past events after the outcomes are known', *Psychological Bulletin*, 107: 311–27.

26 R. Hastie, D. A. Schkade and J. W. Payne (1999), 'Juror judgments in civil cases: hindsight effects on judgments of liability for punitive damages', *Law and Human Behavior*, 23: 597–614.

27 B. L. Schwartz (1998), 'Illusory tip-of-the-tongue states', *Memory*, 6: 623–42.

28 R. Cohen (1991), 'No time for hubris', *Washington Post*, 28 February.

Chapter 6: The Secretive Brain

1 J. A. Bargh and T. L. Chartrand (1999), 'The unbearable automaticity of being', *American Psychologist*, 54: 462–79.

2 See J. A. Bargh and K. Barndollar (1996), 'Automaticity in action: the unconscious as repository of chronic goals and motives', in P. M. Gollwitzer and J. A. Bargh (eds), *The psychology of action: linking cognition and motivation to behavior*, New York: The Guilford Press.

3 G. M. Fitzsimons and J. A. Bargh (2003), 'Thinking of you: nonconscious pursuit of interpersonal goals associated with relationship partners', *Journal of Personality and Social Psychology*, 84: 148–64.

4 D. T. Gilbert and J. G. Hixon (1991), 'The trouble of thinking: activation and application of stereotypes', *Journal of Personality and Social Psychology*, 68: 509–17.

5 J. Shah (2003), 'Automatic for the people: how representations of significant others implicitly affect goal pursuit', *Journal of Personality and Social Psychology*, 84: 661–81.

6 G. M. Fitzsimons and J. A. Bargh (2003), 'Thinking of you: nonconscious pursuit of interpersonal goals associated with relationship partners', *Journal of Personality and Social Psychology*, 84: 148–64.

7 J. A. Bargh, M. Chen and L. Burrows (1996), 'Automaticity of social behavior: direct effects of trait construct and stereotype activation on action', *Journal of Personality and Social Psychology*, 71: 230–44.

8 A. Dijksterhuis and A. van Knippenberg (1998), 'The relation between perception and behavior, or how to win a game of Trivial Pursuit', *Journal of Personality and Social Psychology*, 74: 865–77.

9 J. A. Bargh, M. Chen and L. Burrows (1996), 'Automaticity of social behavior: direct effects of trait construct and stereotype activation on action', *Journal of Personality and Social Psychology*, 71: 230–44.

10 T. E. Moore (1982), 'Subliminal advertising: what you see is what you get', *Journal of Marketing*, 46: 38–47.

11 For discussion of the role of priming in consumer research, see J. A. Bargh (2002), 'Losing consciousness: automatic influences on

consumer judgment, behavior, and motivation', *Journal of Consumer Research*, 29: 280–5.

12 K.C. Berridge and P. Winkielman (2003), 'What is an unconscious emotion? (The case for unconscious "liking")', *Cognition and Emotion*, 17: 181–211.

13 E.J. Strahan, S.J. Spencer and M.P. Zanna (2002), 'Subliminal priming and persuasion: striking while the iron is hot', *Journal of Experimental Social Psychology*, 38: 556–68.

14 J. Cooper and G. Cooper (2002), 'Subliminal motivation: a story revisited', *Journal of Applied Social Psychology*, 32: 2213–27.

15 I.S. Johnsrude, A.M. Owen, N.M. White, W.V. Zhao and V. Bohbot (2000), 'Impaired preference conditioning after anterior temporal lobe resection in humans', *Journal of Neuroscience*, 20: 2649–56. For the classic paper on this subject, see also R.E. Nisbett and T.D. Wilson (1977), 'Telling more than we can know: Verbal reports on mental processes', *Psychological Review*, 84: 231–59.

16 P.G. Zimbardo (1999), 'Discontinuity theory: cognitive and social searches for rationality and normality – may lead to madness', in M.P. Zanna (ed), *Advances in Experimental Social Psychology*, 31: 345–486.

17 D.J. Bem (1972), 'Self-perception theory', in L. Berkowitz (ed), *Advances in Experimental Social Psychology*, 6: 1–62.

18 M.R. Lepper, D. Greene and R.E. Nisbett (1973), 'Undermining children's intrinsic interest with extrinsic reward: a test of the over-justification hypothesis', *Journal of Personality and Social Psychology*, 28: 129–37.

19 D.M. Wegner (2002), *The illusion of conscious will*, Cambridge, MA: MIT Press. See also D.M. Wegner (2003), 'The mind's best trick: how we experience conscious will', *Trends in Cognitive Sciences*, 7: 65–9.

20 B. Libet, C.A. Gleason, E.W. Wright and D.K. Pearl (1983), 'Time of conscious intention to act in relation to onset of cerebral activities (readiness-potential): the unconscious initiation of a freely voluntary act', *Brain*, 106: 623–42. For further discussion of this study, see

B. Libet (1985), 'Unconscious cerebral initiative and the role of conscious will in voluntary action', *Behavioral and Brain Sciences*, 8: 529–66.

21 B. Libet (1999), 'Do we have free will?' *Journal of Consciousness Studies*, 6: 47–57.

CHAPTER 7: The Weak-willed Brain

1 R. F. Baumeister and J. J. Exline (1999), 'Virtue, personality, and social relations: self-control as the moral muscle', *Journal of Personality*, 67: 1165–94.

2 R. F. Baumeister, E. Bratslavsky, M. Muraven and D. M. Tice (1998), 'Ego depletion: Is the active self a limited resource?', *Journal of Personality and Social Psychology*, 74: 1252–65.

3 R. F. Baumeister, E. Bratslavsky, M. Muraven and D. M. Tice (1998), ibid. The authors were particularly interested in the effect of ego depletion on active versus passive responses, and this is where the strongest effect was found.

4 R. F. Baumeister, E. Bratslavsky, M. Muraven and D. M. Tice (1998), ibid; B. J. Schmeichel, K. D. Vohs and R. F. Baumeister (2003), 'Intellectual performance and ego depletion: role of the self in logical reasoning and other information processing', *Journal of Personality and Social Psychology*, 85: 33–46.

5 K. D. Vohs, R. F. Baumeister and N. J. Ciarocco (2005), 'Self-regulation and self-presentation: regulatory resource depletion impairs impression management and effortful self-presentation depletes regulatory resources', *Journal of Personality and Social Psychology*, 88: 632–57.

6 As assessed by various questionnaire measures. K. D. Vohs, R. F. Baumeister and N.J. Ciarocco (2005), ibid.

7 D. M. Tice, E. Bratslavsky and R.F. Baumeister (2001), 'Emotional distress regulation takes precedence over impulse control: if you feel bad, do it!', *Journal of Personality and Social Psychology*, 80: 53–67.

8 D. M. Tice, E. Bratslavsky and R. F. Baumeister (2001), ibid.

9 R. F. Baumeister, C. N. DeWall, N. J. Ciarocco and J. M. Twenge (2005), 'Social exclusion impairs self-regulation', *Journal of Personality and Social Psychology*, 88: 589–604.

10 This was also confirmed statistically using mediation analyses.

11 'My third maxim was to endeavor always to conquer myself rather than the order of the world, and in general accustom myself to the persuasion that except our own thoughts there is nothing absolutely in our power.' René Descartes (*Discourse on Method* Part III). Quoted by D. M. Wegner (1997), 'When the antidote is the poison: ironic mental control processes', *Psychological Science*, 8: 148–50.

12 See, for example, D. M. Wegner (1994), 'Ironic processes of mental control', *Psychological Review*, 101: 34–52.

13 M. E. Ansfield, D. M. Wegner and R. Bowser (1996), 'Ironic effects of sleep urgency', *Behavioural Research and Therapy*, 34: 523–31.

14 R. Ferraro, B. Shiv and J. R. Bettman (2005), 'Let us eat and drink, for tomorrow we shall die: effects of mortality salience and self-esteem on self-regulation in consumer choice', *Journal of Consumer Research* 32: 65–75.

15 M. Muraven, R. F. Baumeister and D. M. Tice (1999), 'Longitudinal improvement of self-regulation through practice: building self-control strength through repeated exercise', *The Journal of Social Psychology*, 139: 446–57.

16 See D. M. Wegner, D. J. Schneider, S. R. Carter and T. L. White (1987), 'Paradoxical effects of thought suppression', *Journal of Personality and Social Psychology*, 53: 5–13.

17 Two other self-control exercises were used: monitoring and recording eating, and regulating mood. (This latter exercise was not particularly successful in improving self-regulation.)

18 D. M. Wegner (1997), 'When the antidote is the poison: ironic mental control processes', *Psychological Science*, 8: 148–50.

19 See M. E. Ansfield, D. M. Wegner and R. Bowser (1996), 'Ironic effects of sleep urgency', *Behavioural Research and Therapy*, 34: 523–31.

20 A. Fischbach, R. S. Friedman and A. W. Kruglanski (2003), 'Leading

us not into temptation: Momentary allurements elicit overriding goal activation', *Journal of Personality and Social Psychology*, 84: 296–309.

21 A. Fischbach, R. S. Friedman and A. W. Kruglanski (2003), ibid. See study 4.

22 See, for example, P. M. Gollwitzer (1999), 'Implementation intentions: strong effects of simple plans', *American Psychologist*, 54: 493–503.

23 S.E. Milne, S. Orbell and P. Sheeran (2002), 'Combining motivational and volitional interventions to promote exercise participation: Protection motivation theory and implementation intentions', *British Journal of Health Psychology*, 7: 163–84.

24 B. Verplanken and S. Faes (1999), 'Good intentions, bad habits, and effects of forming implementation intentions on healthy eating', *European Journal of Social Psychology*, 29: 591–604; C. J. Armitage (2004), 'Evidence that implementation intentions reduce dietary fat intake: a randomized trial', *Health Psychology*, 23: 319–23; but for contrary finding for healthy-eating behaviours, see C. Jackson, R. Lawton, P. Knapp et al. (2005), 'Beyond intention: do specific plans increase health behaviours in patients in primary care? A study of fruit and vegetable consumption', *Social Science and Medicine*, 60: 2383–91; R. W. Holland, H. Aarts and D. Landendam (2006), 'Breaking and creating habits on the working floor: A field experiment on the power of implementation intentions', *Journal of Experimental Social Psychology*, 42: 776–83; S. Koole and M. Spijker (2000), 'Overcoming the planning fallacy through willpower: effects of implementation intentions on actual and predicted task-completion times', *European Journal of Social Psychology*, 30: 873–88; S. Orbell, S. Hodgkins and P. Sheeran (1997), 'Implementation intentions and the theory of planned behavior', *Personality and Social Psychology Bulletin*, 23: 945–54.

25 D. Lavin and A. Groarke (2005), 'Dental floss behaviour: a test of the predictive utility of the Theory of Planned Behaviour and the effects of making implementation intentions', *Psychology, Health and Medicine*, 10: 243–52.

CHAPTER 8: **The Bigoted Brain**

1 P. Devine (1989), 'Stereotypes and prejudice: their automatic and controlled components', *Journal of Personality and Social Psychology*, 56: 5–18.

2 Most research investigating the effects of the black stereotype on perception and behaviour has used non-black participants. However, stigmatised groups are aware of the stereotypes that exist about themselves, and there is evidence that, at an unconscious level, they have a similar bias against their own group. For a useful discussion and data, see A.R. Greenwald and L. Hamilton Krieger (2006), 'Implicit bias: Scientific foundations', *California Law Review*, 94: 945–67. See also Correll et al. (2002), 'The police officer's dilemma: Using ethnicity to disambiguate potentially threatening individuals', *Journal of Personality and Social Psychology*, 83: 1314–29, which is discussed later in the chapter.

3 K.B. Payne (2001), 'Prejudice and perception: the role of automatic and controlled processes in misperceiving a weapon', *Journal of Personality and Social Psychology*, 81: 181–92.

4 J. Correll, B. Park, C.M. Judd and B. Wittenbrink (2002), 'The police officer's dilemma: using ethnicity to disambiguate potentially threatening individuals', *Journal of Personality and Social Psychology*, 83: 1314–29.

5 E.A. Plant and B.M. Peruche (2005), 'The consequences of race for police officers' responses to criminal suspects', *Psychological Science*, 16: 180–3.

6 L. Lepore and R. Brown (1997), 'Category and stereotype activation: is prejudice inevitable?', *Journal of Personality and Social Psychology*, 72: 275–87.

7 L.A. Rudman and E. Borgida (1995), 'The afterglow of construct accessibility: the behavioral consequences of priming men to view women as sexual objects', *Journal of Experimental Social Psychology*, 31: 493–517.

8 J.A. Bargh, M. Chen and L. Burrows (1996), 'Automaticity of social

behavior: direct effects of trait construct and stereotype activation on action', *Journal of Personality and Social Psychology*, 71: 230–44.

9   M. Chen and J. A. Bargh (1997), 'Nonconscious behavioral confirmation processes: the self-fulfilling consequences of automatic stereotype activation', *Journal of Experimental Social Psychology*, 33: 541–60.

10 C. O. Word, M. P. Zanna and J. Cooper (1974), 'The nonverbal mediation of self-fulfilling prophecies in interracial interaction', *Journal of Experimental Social Psychology*, 10: 109–20.

11 T. K. Vescio, S. J. Gervais, M. Snyder and A. Hoover (2005), 'Power and the creation of patronizing environments: the stereotype-based behaviors of the powerful and their effects on female performance in masculine domains', *Journal of Personality and Social Psychology*, 88: 658–72.

12 These results were obtained when men were encouraged to take a 'weakness-based' approach to leadership (to focus on weaknesses that might thwart a team's chances of success). Men encouraged to take the contrary 'strength-based' approach treated men and women equally, as did women team leaders in both 'weakness-based' and 'strength-based' conditions.

13 See C. M. Steele (1997), 'A threat in the air: how stereotypes shape intellectual identity and performance', *American Psychologist*, 52: 613–29.

14 S. J. Spencer, C. M. Steele and D. M. Quin (1999), 'Stereotype threat and women's math performance', *Journal of Experimental Social Psychology*, 35: 4–28.

15 M. Johns, T. Schmader and A. Martens (2005), 'Knowing is half the battle: teaching stereotype threat as a means of improving women's math performance', *Psychological Science*, 16: 175–9.

16 Unpublished manuscript of J. Aronson and J. Williams (2004), cited by M. Johns, T. Schmader and A. Martens (2005), ibid.

17 G. M. Walton and G. L. Cohen (2003), 'Stereotype lift', *Journal of Experimental Social Psychology*, 39: 456–67.

18 See L. Jussim (1991), 'Social perception and social reality: a reflection-construction model', *Psychological Review*, 98: 54–73.

19 A. Marcus-Newhall, S. Thompson and C. Thomas (2001), 'Examining a gender stereotype: menopausal women', *Journal of Applied Social Psychology*, 31: 695–719.

20 Z. Kunda and K. C. Oleson (1995), 'Maintaining stereotypes in the face of disconfirmation: constructing grounds for subtyping deviants', *Journal of Personality and Social Psychology*, 68: 565–79.

21 Z. Kunda and K. C. Oleson (1997), 'When exceptions prove the rule: how extremity of deviance determines the impact of deviant examples on stereotypes', *Journal of Personality and Social Psychology*, 72: 965–79.

22 L. A. Rudman and K. Fairchild (2004), 'Reactions to counterstereotypic behavior: the role of backlash in cultural stereotype maintenance', *Journal of Personality and Social Psychology*, 87: 157–76.

23 L. A. Rudman and P. Glick (1999), 'Feminized management and backlash toward agentic women: the hidden costs to women of a kinder, gentler image of middle managers', *Journal of Personality and Social Psychology*, 77: 743–62.

24 L. A. Rudman (1998), 'Self-promotion as a risk factor for women: the costs and benefits of counterstereotypical impression management', *Journal of Personality and Social Psychology*, 74: 629–45.

25 P. Glick and S. T. Fiske (2001), 'An ambivalent alliance: hostile and benevolent sexism as complementary justifications for gender inequality', *American Psychologist*, 56: 109–18.

26 'The ideological rationalization that men and women hold complementary but equal positions in society appears to be a fairly recent invention. In earlier times – and in more conservative company today – it was not felt necessary to provide the ideology with an equalitarian veneer.' S. L. Bem and D. J. Bem (1970), quoted in J. T. Jost and A. C. Kay (2005), 'Exposure to benevolent sexism and complementary gender stereotypes: Consequences for specific and diffuse forms of system justification', *Journal of Personality and Social Psychology*, 88: 298–509.

27 See P. Glick and S.T. Fiske (2001), 'An ambivalent alliance: hostile and benevolent sexism as complementary justifications for gender inequality', *American Psychologist*, 56: 109–18. In the four most sexist nations of the nineteen that they studied (as assessed by two United Nations cross-national indices of gender inequality), women endorsed benevolent sexism even more strongly than did men. (The countries were Cuba, Nigeria, South Africa and Botswana).

28 J.T. Jost and A.C. Kay (2005), 'Exposure to benevolent sexism and complementary gender stereotypes: consequences for specific and diffuse forms of system justification', *Journal of Personality and Social Psychology*, 88: 498–509.

29 L. Sinclair and Z. Kunda (1999), 'Reactions to a black professional: motivated inhibition and activation of conflicting stereotypes', *Journal of Personality and Social Psychology*, 77: 885–904; L. Sinclair and Z. Kunda (2000), 'Motivated stereotyping of women: she's fine if she praised me but incompetent if she criticized me', *Personality and Social Psychology Bulletin*, 26: 1329–42.

30 S. Fein and S.J. Spencer (1997), 'Prejudice as self-image maintenance: affirming the self through derogating others', *Journal of Personality and Social Psychology*, 73: 31–44.

31 See Z. Kunda and S.J. Spencer (2003), 'When do stereotypes come to mind and when do they color judgment? A goal-based theoretical framework for stereotype activation and application', *Psychological Bulletin*, 129 : 522–44.

32 M.J. Monteith and C.I. Voils (1998), 'Proneness to prejudiced responses: toward understanding the authenticity of self-reported discrepancies', *Journal of Personality and Social Psychology*, 75: 901–16.

33 B. Monin and D.T. Miller (2001), 'Moral credentials and the expression of prejudice', *Journal of Personality and Social Psychology*, 81: 5–16.

34 C.N. Macrae, G.V. Bodenhausen, A.B. Milne and J. Jetten (1994), 'Out of mind but back in sight: stereotypes on the rebound', *Journal of Personality and Social Psychology*, 67: 808–17.

35 See M. J. Monteith, J. W. Sherman and P. Devine (1998), 'Suppression as a stereotype control strategy', *Personality and Social Psychology Review*, 2: 63–82.

36 C. N. Macrae, A. B. Milne and G. V. Bodenhausen (1994), 'Stereotypes as energy-saving devices: a peek inside the cognitive toolbox', *Journal of Personality and Social Psychology*, 66: 37–47.

37 See M. J. Monteith (1993), 'Self-regulation of prejudiced responses: implications for progress in prejudice-reduction efforts', *Journal of Personality and Social Psychology*, 65: 469–85; M. J. Monteith, L. Ashburn-Nardo, C. I. Voils and A. M. Czopp (2002), 'Putting the brakes on prejudice: on the development and operation of cues for control', *Journal of Personality and Social Psychology*, 83: 1029–50.

38 P. M. Gollwitzer, B. Schaal, G. B. Moskowitz, H. J. P. Hammelbeck and W. Wasel (1999), 'Implementation intention effects on stereotype and prejudice activation', cited in P. M. Gollwitzer, 'Implementation intentions: Strong effects of simple plans', *American Psychologist*, 54: 493–503.

EPILOGUE: The Vulnerable Brain

1 See motivated scepticism as described in Chapter 1, pp. 16–18.

2 See belief perseverance and susceptibility to innuendo as described in Chapter 5, pp. 114–19 and 120–1.

3 S. Lewandowsky, W. G. K. Stritzke, K. Oberauer and M. Morales (2005), 'Memory for fact, fiction, and misinformation: the Iraq War 2003', *Psychological Science*, 16: 190–5.

4 See emotional contagion of moral judgments as described in Chapter 3, pp. 56–7. This particular case is described in L. H. Colwell (2005), 'Cognitive heuristics in the context of legal decision making', *American Journal of Forensic Psychology*, 23: 17–41.

5 How did the hypothesis (now completely discredited) that 'refrigerator mothers' were responsible for autism in their children come to hold such great sway in the 1950s and 1960s? Could it have been, in part, because of our need to believe in a just world ('bad things

happen to bad people')? See Chapter 3, pp. 38–62, and illusory correlation as described in Chapter 4, pp. 82–5.

6   See situational control of behaviour and the correspondence bias as described in Chapter 3, pp. 71–2. See also the effects of stress, distraction, social exclusion, etc., on willpower as described in Chapter 7.

7   See biased interpretation of ambiguous behaviour as described in Chapter 8. Regarding the use of stereotypes in making tacit inferences, see D. Dunning and D. A. Sherman (1997), 'Stereotypes and tacit inference', *Journal of Personality and Social Psychology*, 73: 459–71.

8   In a detailed analysis of the peer review process of the Swedish Medical Research Council, researchers found that women scientists had to be about two and a half times more productive than their male counterparts in order to be considered as competent a scientist. C. Wennerås and A. Wold (1997), 'Nepotism and sexism in peer review', *Nature*, 387: 341–3.

9   See the role of racial stereotypes in perception as described in Chapter 8, pp. 180–2.

10 See emotion-congruent judgments as described in Chapter 2, pp. 38–41.

11 See post hoc and erroneous explanations of behaviour as described in Chapter 6, pp. 137–42. Wilson and Nisbett found that shoppers, presented with four pairs of identical stockings, disproportionately preferred those presented on the right. (Needless to say, the shoppers did not cite position as a factor in their preference for a particular stocking.) See T. D. Wilson and R. E. Nisbett (1978), 'The accuracy of verbal reports about the effects of stimuli on evaluations and behavior', *Social Psychology*, 41: 118–31.

12 B. W. Pelham, M. C. Mirenberg and J. T. Jones (2002), 'Why Susie sells seashells by the seashore: implicit egotism and major life decisions', *Journal of Personality and Social Psychology*, 82: 469–87; J. T. Jones, B. W. Pelham, M. Carvallo and M. C. Mirenberg (2004), 'How do I love thee? Let me count the Js: Implicit egotism and interpersonal attraction', *Journal of Personality and Social Psychology*, 87: 665–83.

13 See the effect of schema priming on behaviour as described in Chapter 6, pp. 130–6.

14 Regarding these and subsequent examples, see the effect on behaviour of negative or benevolent stereotypes as described in Chapter 8.

15 But not if the goal was presented as being socially unacceptable. H. Aarts, P.M. Gollwitzer and R.R. Hassin (2004), 'Goal contagion: perceiving is for pursuing', *Journal of Personality and Social Psychology*, 87: 23–37.

16 The term 'mental contamination' defined by T.D. Wilson and N. Brekke (1994), 'Mental contamination and mental correction: unwanted influences on judgments and evaluations', *Psychological Bulletin*, 116: 117–42. They discuss strategies for avoiding mental contamination.

17 See the 'you can't not believe everything you read' phenomenon as described in Chapter 5, pp. 119–20.

18 See Chapter 2, p. 40.

19 See T.D. Wilson and N. Brekke (1994), 'Mental contamination and mental correction: unwanted influences on judgments and evaluations', *Psychological Bulletin*, 116: 117–42.

20 For example, volunteers made accountable for the judgments of the culpability of defendants avoided the biasing effects of carry-over anger. See Chapter 3, p. 57. Also see E.P. Thompson, G.B. Moskowitz, S. Chaiken and J.A. Bargh (1994), 'Accuracy motivation attenuates covert priming: the systematic reprocessing of social information', *Journal of Personality and Social Psychology*, 66: 474–89.

21 For example, people think that the self-serving bias affects other people more than it does themselves. See Chapter 1, p. x; Also, people think that situational factors will influence their own behaviour less than it does other people's. See Chapter 3, pp. 70–1.

Index